THE CHALLENGE OF LIGHT TACKLE

THE CHALLENGE OF LIGHT TACKLE

LINDSEY GREEN

BLANDFORD

I dedicate this book to my wife, Julie, and to my children
Anthony, Rebecca and Charlotte.

A BLANDFORD BOOK

First published in the UK 1995
by Blandford
A Cassell Imprint
Wellington House
125 Strand
LONDON
WC2R 0BB

Distributed in the United States by Sterling Publishing Co., Inc.
387 Park Avenue South, New York, NY 10016-8810

Distributed in Australia by Capricorn Link (Australia) Pty Ltd
2/13 Carrington Road, Castle Hill, NSW 2154

British Library Cataloguing-in-Publication Data
A catalogue record for this book is available from the British Library.

ISBN 0-7137-2429-3 (hardback)
ISBN 0-7137-2538-9 (paperback)

Typeset by MS Filmsetting Limited, Frome, Somerset
Printed and bound in Great Britain by The Bath Press, Avon

CONTENTS

ACKNOWLEDGEMENTS

I would like to thank all the people who contributed their valuable time and practical assistance while I was researching *The Challenge of Light Tackle*. In particular I would like to thank both Diane Sollis of DAM (UK) Ltd and Chris Leibbrandt of Ryobi Tackle for the encouragement and support that they have given many of the junior or disabled anglers with whom I am acquainted. I would also like to thank Tony Cuthbertson from Normark and Nick Young from the Leeda Group for the help and information that they supplied.

Lindsey Green

FOREWORD

Fishing with light tackle is becoming more popular by the day. Anglers are experiencing the thrill of playing fish where the odds are at best evens and in many cases better for the fish. Lindsey Green long ago found this out and has fished 'light' for many years. His experiments have led him to examine how coarse anglers fish and he has adapted some of their tackle and methods, including the pole.

His interest in this form of fishing is being transferred to the juniors of the Torbay Association of Sea Anglers, where he is in charge of the junior section. He teaches them on the local shores and they are now growing up to enjoy the sport of sea-fishing. His instruction booklets on tackle, knots and rigs are much sought after by the youngsters.

This book leads the beginner through the maze not only explaining how, why and where to use light tackle but also imparting the thrill of the catch, through the eyes of the author and his children. It exudes the same enthusiasm for fishing as his two previous books in this series and will do much to encourage all anglers, not only beginners, to try light-tackle fishing. I am sure, before the last page is reached, that even old hands will have had their appetites whetted and be longing to have a go.

Ted Tuckerman

CHAPTER ONE

A SPORTING CHANCE

Glancing upwards, he could see the prey silhouetted against the early light of morning, its movements growing increasingly more frantic as it sensed the approach of danger from underneath. It darted left, circled, then turned over on its side as it circled once again, moving higher in the water in a futile attempt to escape.

Glancing downwards, the angler noted the slight bobbing of the float as it tilted first one way, then the other. Cautious fingers silently eased the bail arm over, then softly picked up the slack in preparation for the strike.

Suddenly, with no further warning, the float tilted over and was drawn diagonally through the water. The angler watched its rapid descent and then, at the count of three, swept the rod tip aloft, setting the hook firmly in his opponent's mouth. The bass reacted both angrily and decisively, turning and cutting through the water with such power that the rod arched over and the reel sang as its line was paid out against the drag.

Feeling the strength of the fish, the angler cautiously extended the rod, placing side-strain upon it in an effort to turn the fish and guide it closer. For a few seconds more the bass ran, before turning abruptly and swimming towards the angler, shaking its head as it tried to dislodge the hook. For a moment it looked as though this tactic would work, but then the angler ran backwards himself, reeling line frantically until he was once again in contact with the fish.

Feeling the sudden return of that irritating pressure, the bass turned and swam backwards and forwards, its movements anticipated and matched by the angler until, at last, it was drawn towards the net. Then, realizing its imminent danger, the great bass turned and frantically swam away from the menacing object. Its flight was controlled and once more it found itself being led towards the waiting net. It tried to flee once again, and again, but each time, as it tired, so it was drawn closer until it found itself wrapped in the folds of the mesh as the angler triumphantly swept it ashore.

Grinning, as excited as a little boy, the angler knelt beside the bass, turning it gently as his forceps deftly removed the hook from its mouth. Then, carefully avoiding both the gill covers and its spiny dorsal fin, he picked up the fish, weighed it, then held it in the water, gently supporting it until it recovered sufficiently to swim away. Then the angler rose, wiped his hands and gently picked up the rod that he was using, the delicate but power-ful wand that had reacted so well to the challenge of a few moments before, the chal-lenge of light tackle.

*　*　*

Twenty years ago, as a teenager growing up in Torbay, I watched that thrilling scene with both excitement and envy. It was, for me, the start of a fascination with light tackle that has never waned; indeed it has grown until I am as convinced today as I was then that it is very much the way forward in developing

An evening run of mackerel gave these two anglers some very good sport.

saltwater-angling as a sport. It has so much to offer, especially nowadays when, with such rapid advances in technology, the angler has a wider range of equipment at his disposal than at any time in the past.

The angler who is prepared to experiment with lighter tackle has significant advantages over his conventional contemporaries. One of these is the sheer quality of the sport that he or she can enjoy. A mackerel struggling gamely on a match rod fights with an abandon that would amaze the man with beachcaster and feathers. Garfish, leaping athletically from the water, fight out of all proportion to their size. Nor are they alone. Bass, pollack, mullet, flatfish, scad, John Dories and any number of other fish will all shine in a different light if they are caught on appropriate tackle.

So what defines appropriate tackle? For me it is the lightest possible outfit you can get away with, covering anything from single-handed baitcasters to match, fly or carp rods up to a maximum test curve of $2\frac{1}{2}$ lb ($1\cdot1$ kg), possibly 3 lb ($1\cdot4$ kg) if you are after really big bass. You might also like to experiment with poles, which can provide both an exciting and inexpensive introduction to using lighter tackle. As to which outfit or outfits you decide upon, that will depend on the type of fishing available in your area. You will need to have a look at the types of fish to be found locally, gauge the strength of currents carefully and then choose whichever combination appears to be the most versatile and relevant to the part of the country that you fish. For example, in Torbay we are lucky enough to encounter a wide range of species in fairly moderate conditions. There are only a few spots where we really need to use larger weights and heavier tackle, which has meant that local anglers can really go to town and experiment. The results have been very good, with different outfits proving themselves in a variety of situations.

Probably the most versatile and widely adopted combination has been a carp rod and light, fixed-spool reel for catching mackerel, bass, pollack, garfish, dogfish and whiting,

with the outfit capable of being used for both float-fishing and legering. Baitcasters and light multipliers have similar applications, although their legering capabilities are limited, and they have the added advantage of being an ideal length to double up for both inshore boatwork and spinning, where the fight you can get from a reasonable fish just has to be experienced to be believed! Fly rods can provide some spectacular sport with mackerel, bass, scad, pollack and herring − particularly at the mouths of estuaries − while match rods are ideal for light float-fishing for mullet, mackerel and garfish. Lastly pole-fishing, despite its obvious limitations, can be a very exciting way to fish, and both I and members of my immediate family use them successfully to catch bass, flounders, wrasse, mackerel, garfish and pollack.

Besides simply enhancing the quality of the fight that you get from the fish that you catch, there are several other advantages to using light tackle. Take, for example, legering. It can be really enjoyable casting large weights a significant distance from the shore, but do you always need to? Certainly, if your fishing is based around Weston-super-Mare or Dungeness, then the answer is probably yes, but in any number of other locations then the answer really ought to be no. You could, for example, use a carp rod to cast a 2 oz (57 g) lead up to 100 yd (90 m) from the shore, perhaps even further if you streamline your tackle, and catch just as many fish. You should catch even more. When a fish pulls against a 2 oz (57 g) lead weight he feels much less resistance than if he is brought up short against a spiked lead weighing in excess of 5 oz (142 g). That gives the angler a few extra seconds in which to strike, seconds which could mean the difference between success or failure. The lighter tip of the rod will also signal bites much more clearly than a conventional beachcaster, making them easier to spot and enabling the angler to strike more quickly than might otherwise be the case, especially if the rod is being held rather than put in a rest.

This is, in itself, quite an advantage. You can hold light tackle for long periods without discomfort, being ready to strike instantly the moment that a fish takes your bait. Can you imagine holding a beachcaster for similar periods — say 2 or 3 hours at a stretch? It would be, to say the least, uncomfortable. They were not designed to be fished in that manner. Light tackle was. It may not have the distance available on a beachcaster, but it certainly is far more efficient for short- to medium-range fishing than any beachcaster I have ever used. There is less weight to alarm the fish, resulting in more confident bites, while the bites themselves are much easier to spot and can be struck with a minimum of delay. The resulting fight from each fish is also far more enjoyable than might otherwise be the case.

So why buy beachcasters at all? There are only two reasons why a beachcaster will outperform lighter tackle. The first of these is where considerable distance — say over 125 yd (115 m) — is essential to put you among fish and the second is to anchor your tackle in a tidal flow too fast for a 2 oz (57 g) spiked weight. If these conditions apply, then well and good, I would be the first person to reach

A pollack taken on a pole. Prawns are often a good bait for this species.

for such a rod. If they don't, then lighter tackle makes much better sense. The trouble is that beachcasters have been taking over shore-fishing to the exclusion of anything else. People have become brainwashed into the mistaken belief that greater distance equals better fishing. This may be true sometimes, but it is more often not the case. Many a time I have watched people casting over the spots where I would expect the fish to be, sometimes well beyond where the fish have congregated. They have moaned a great deal about there being no fish to catch and have then been surprised as my children and I have reeled in fish from virtually under their noses. The fact is that beachcasters are not an ideal solution to every spot you are ever likely to fish. If you analyse your marks, then the chances are that you will find that beachcasters are only essential for some 5 to 10 per cent of available time in the summer, rising to 50 per cent in the winter. The rest of the time would be more profitably spent using much lighter gear.

There is also another advantage to using lighter tackle – its price. You can get a superb outfit, both rod and reel, for less than the price of a good beachcaster on its own. In fact, if you shopped around carefully, you could really surprise yourself with just how cheap decent rods and reels can be. It depends, of course, on both your tastes and the locations that you are going to fish but you might, for example, pick up a decent carp rod and matching fixed-spool reel for under £70, well under the asking price for a reasonable beachcaster. Telescopic poles can be bought for less than £20 and baitcasters, when they are available, will set you back in the region of £40 for the rod and somewhat more for a light multiplier to match.

All in all, light tackle has much to offer the angler. I hope you will be tempted to experiment for yourself, so you can discover first-hand both the excitement and rewards of using lighter tackle. After all, what have you got to lose? With the current intense commercial pressure on fish stocks it is unlikely that we will suddenly find a dramatic increase in the average size of the fish that we are catching. The opposite is far more likely, in which case does it not make sense to maximize our opportunities for sport? Light tackle offers the angler the chance to do just that. All things considered it must certainly be worth your while trying it: you may surprise yourself!

CHAPTER TWO

SOME TACKLE TO START

One of the joys of light tackle is the sheer diversity of the outfits that you can use. Unlike beachcasting, where the tackle is more or less the same, there is such a range of rods and reels available that the purist can experiment to his or her heart's content, scaling down both tackle and approach in order to maximize the opportunities for enjoyment. The only problem is deciding which outfit or outfits to choose. There is such an enormous selection available that you can spend a fortune very easily, especially if you live in an area like Torbay, where the currents are generally mild and you can get away with using much lighter weights. This is important because the lighter the leads, the lighter and more varied the tackle that you will be able to use.

Instead of sticking to beachcasters you might like to experiment with light floats on a match rod, legering with spinning or carp rods, fly-fishing, drifting or spinning with baitcasters, long-distance floating on a feeder rod or even dispensing with a reel altogether and just dropping your tackle down at the end of a pole. The results are electric. Each and every outfit will reward you with a degree of sport that you will never touch on a beachcaster. Fish that you will hardly feel on a conventional rod will turn and fight with a vigour that seems to transform them into a different species, fighting all the way in instead of simply being winched ashore.

The only problem is deciding where to start. Some people seem to go the whole hog, buying everything in one go, but in my opinion it is far better to start in a modest way and then collect other equipment as you get used to this style of fishing. Once you start experimenting you will soon find that your whole approach undergoes a radical and very positive change, which can mean that what suits you at the outset may very well be abandoned as your quest for personal excellence takes over. It is far better to dip your toe first, choosing an outfit which you will be able to use for as wide a variety of applications as possible, and then to expand your range of tackle as your experience widens.

So where do you begin? The first step is to look at your local shoreline and see what species are available throughout the year. As you do so you will very quickly come to realize that these are strongly influenced by the season. Where I live, for example, we have a major influx of summer species which seem to arrive in several waves, especially in the case of mackerel. One reason for this is that Torbay lies on the migratory routes of two separate and distinct stocks. The result is a first wave of mackerel entering our waters about halfway through March and almost totally disappearing in the space of a fortnight, followed in early May by a second wave, which will take up residence until much later in the season. We have much the same situation with other species, giving us a quality of sport which is virtually consistent throughout the year. You can nearly always catch something, somewhere, as long as you have the right tackle and bait.

In January you might be legering for flounders or dogfish, or using very light float tackle for whiting or pollack. In February — our leanest month — you might end up fishing almost exclusively for dogfish and whiting, with an occasional bull huss making an appearance. If you can get afloat in March and April, then the early run of plaice will give you some spectacular sport, while back on the shore the first wave of mackerel kicks the float-fishing season off to a flying start. Then, from May until September, there are so many fish close to shore that you can more or less pick on the species to suit yourself — with the exception of cod and coalfish. Dogfish seem to disappear for a while during April and May, but there are so many other species available that it really doesn't matter. Then, in October and November, we have a change-over time which can sometimes last right up until Christmas. During this time you can experiment with such a variety of tackle that nearly any method seems to produce something, provided that you persevere and make sure that your bait is the best that you can get hold of.

With such an abundance of species, including bass, pollack, mackerel, flatfish, wrasse, garfish and mullet, to name but a few, it quickly becomes obvious that there is tremendous scope for experiment. Add to this the light currents and the fact that each species has its own idiosyncrasies and you can see why anyone can diversify as widely as they like. We are very lucky; any or all of the outfits that I have mentioned can be used to catch a variety of species. You can pick whatever takes your fancy and have a good chance of catching fish. However, if we were less fortunate, then it would make more sense to start with an outfit tailored to the area. This would be chosen according to the geography of the area in question, the species that are available and the strength of the currents. If these factors prove restrictive, you may find yourself looking at only a few outfits, in which case it makes sense to have a pretty good idea of their capabilities before you spend any money.

To help you with this I am going to mention some useful outfits and list some of the ways in which they may be used, together with the conditions required in order to ensure a reasonable likelihood of success. In this way you can narrow down the selection to those that are suited to the area where you live. Before I do this, however, I must spend a few moments looking at reels and their applications. There are far more reels available for light tackle than there are for conventional beachcasters, so it will pay you briefly to familiarize yourself with the types that I am going to mention. I would not worry too much about actual models at this stage as it is more important to know what they *do* rather than look at individual and specific differences from model to model. I will, however, put a short list after each section, naming reels which I have found to be reliable over at least several months of regular use. You may or may not find this helpful, but it should at least give you a starting point when you come to choose your own.

REELS

Multipliers

The first reels I am going to mention are multipliers. These are so-named because the gears have been arranged to make the spool go round several times for every turn of the handle. They are perhaps the hardest reels to learn to use, but they are also the smoothest. If you persevere and do not allow yourself to be distracted by any tangles, you will eventually find that their silky-smooth performance is excellent for handling any fish that you catch. The only minor drawbacks are that they are relatively slow to wind-in and that you can get a few tangles while you are learning to cast them. They are, however, some of the best reels you will ever encounter for light-tackle applications, especially the lighter, palm-sized multipliers known as 'baitcasters'. These are deliberately very small, but are usually quite sophisticated with magnetic casting controls. Their spool capacity is also admirably suited to lighter lines because, although they appear to be tiny, they are usually capable of taking 150 yd (135 m) of 8 lb (3·6 kg) breaking-strain line, which is ample. The result is a reel which is comfortable to hold but still man enough to tackle most of the species that you are ever likely to encounter. They are ideal for long-distance casting or situations where you are going to be repeatedly casting, such as spinning. They are also very useful for inshore boat-fishing.

If you do a lot of beachcasting, then the chances are that you will probably already own a multiplier like the ABU Ambassadeur 6500 C3 or a close equivalent. These work just as well on lighter rods as they do on the heavier ones and are particularly suitable for bass-fishing from both boat or shore. They are perfectly suitable for inshore boatwork and are a sound investment for anyone just starting, although you might like to drop the size down to a slightly smaller model. It depends on whether or not you want the reel to double-up for beachcasting as well as using it with your lighter gear. If so, it will probably pay you to invest in a spare spool and keep one loaded with lighter line. If you only want it for light tackle then you might like to scale the reel down to perhaps an Ambassadeur 5000 or

The ABU Ambassadeur Maxxar, a well-designed baitcasting reel.

equivalent. There is quite a range to choose from so you should very easily be able to find something that you particularly like.

I wish I could say the same thing about baitcasters. Unfortunately these are much more difficult to get hold of and you may even find yourself having to order one specially. It is to be hoped that more models will become available as British anglers realize just how good they are but, at the present time, the field is quite limited. I tried out two models – the Ambassadeur Maxxar and the Ryobi T20 – and gave both of them a real pasting. They performed extremely well, although I would stress that these are really specialist reels which work best with rods fitted with a trigger-grip reel seat. Matched with the right rod they are a sheer delight to handle but, if you mismatch the rod, you will be wasting your money. Get the right tool for the job and

then try them out. You may well find yourself – as I did – becoming virtually addicted to the sport they can offer.

Fixed-spool Reels
Probably the most popular type of reel for light-tackle work at the moment is the fixed spool. This is a reel in which the spool has been located at the front of the reel. The spool itself does not rotate – although it may give line out under pressure – but remains fixed in position while a line-collection device – the bail arm – is turned around the spool, thereby winding the line onto it. The rate of retrieve is much faster than for most multipliers, but the retrieve under pressure is nowhere near as smooth. They are built to take a lot of punishment and are also relatively cheap, with a quality model costing quite a bit less than the equivalent multiplier. They are easy to

The Ryobi T20 is a no-nonsense baitcaster which is easy to use.

LOADING LINE ONTO A FIXED-SPOOL REEL

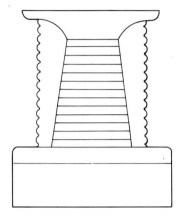

(1) An underfilled spool will reduce the distance which you can cast.

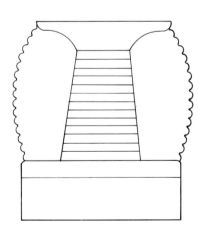

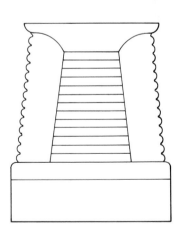

(2) An overfilled spool will result in tangled line.

(3) In this correctly filled spool the line is almost but not quite level with the rim.

cast, faster for winding-in — which is important when you are trying to clear any obstructions in the water — and easy to handle. You can cast a long way quite easily, especially with the extended or conical spools, and will encounter

The Ryobi XLR 200 is a rear-drag fixed spool with a quick-release button on the spool. This is useful if you need to sort out any tangles. It also comes in handy if you forget to put the line under the bail arm!

few problems, but it is important that you remember to fill the spool so that the line is almost, but not quite, level with the rim. If you overfill with line then you will end up with quite a few tangles but, if you put too little line on, you will cut short the distance that you cast. The diagrams on page 17 should make this clear.

Once you start looking at fixed-spool reels, you will quickly come to realize that there is an enormous range of them on the market. Some of these will advertise the fact that they have a rear drag while others will specify a front drag, both of which have been designed to allow the fish to take line out under pressure rather than snap the line. In practice I would always go for a rear-drag reel. If you have set the drag too high you can reach the rear of the reel quite easily, even in the middle of a fight, and reset it to the right degree of pressure.

If you are using a front-drag reel this is nowhere near as simple. Instead you will have to place your hand over the front of the spool which will interfere with the line coming off the reel. This could easily cost you the fish, which would be a great pity.

If you decide not to look at front-drag reels, then you need not worry about this stipulation unnecessarily narrowing your choice. Most modern reels are now fitted with rear drags and, if I wanted to, I could fill the rest of the chapter with possible options. Obviously I will not do that, but I will list a few of the models that I have tested out, while pointing out that, with these reels, as with everything else, you get what you pay for. I have listed some cheaper models that worked well, but it would be unrealistic to expect these to have the same smoothness of action that characterizes the more expensive fixed spools. Suffice it to say that, in general, the more you spend the better the performance you will obtain in return. Having said that, I gave each of the following reels a really good trial and experienced no problems with any of them. I have listed them according to size and application:

1   Lighter reels for use on very light rods:
    DAM CDi II 325 and 330, CDII 225, LS25
    Camaro LS.

2   Small reels for float-fishing, spinning and
    light legering:
    DAM CDi II 330, CDII 230.
    Ryobi T100 and T200 Target (budget
    reels), Chaser XLR 100.

3   Medium reels for legering and bass:
    Ryobi T300.
    DAM SE140, LS45 Camaro LS (budget),
    CDFS 350 (free-spool), CDi II 340,
    CDII 240, Finessa Spin.

Closed-face Reels

Closed- or open-face reels are similar to fixed
spools except that the spool is partially or
almost completely enclosed and there is a
quick-release button located on either the
front or the rear of the reel. When this button
is depressed, the line is free to tumble off the
spool. They are easy to cast — though not as
long-casting as either fixed spools or multipliers — but they really come into their own for
smooth handling on very fine lines. This is
particularly true of open-faced reels, which are
ideal for use on match rods if you like going
after mullet. I bought an Abumatic 1044
Syncro Match and have had a great deal of fun
with it, especially during the summer months
when I loaded it with 2 lb (0·9 kg) breaking-
strain line and used it for mackerel and garfish.

Closed-face reels have the same smooth
handling as open-face reels, but they don't
handle knotted lines very well. If you have to
join two lengths of line then you will start
getting a lot of problems when you cast. So
long as you do not knot your line — and
frankly, if you do then it is time to get rid of it
anyway — you will find that they are excellent
for spinning and really come into their own
when you match them with pistol-grip baitcasting rods. As for possible models, then I
would suggest that the Abumatic Bronco is
well worth having a look at. It is a good reel at
a very modest price.

*The DAM CD 230 is a smaller fixed spool which
has a very smooth drag, making it a good reel for
mulleting.*

The other point I will mention is the ease
with which you can cast these reels. My
youngest daughter was having a lot of trouble
learning to cast until she saw a very cheap and
cheerful little ABU set in a local shop. The rod
and reel together cost under £20 and,
although they are far from being good quality,
they nonetheless allowed Charlie to start casting a respectable distance at the age of 7 years

The DAM SE140 is a medium fixed-spool reel suitable for going after bass.

— and by 'respectable' I mean that she was casting a float in excess of 60 yd (55 m). The rod was very floppy — it would bend double on a small mackerel — but even so she managed to control the fish that she caught without any significant problems. She had a lot of fun on it and caught some very big mackerel and garfish, each of which put up a tremendous fight. It just goes to show that you should not dismiss any outfit on the basis of cosmetics alone.

You can get hold of closed-face reels and matching rods very cheaply if you shop around and, although some of these look pretty awful, they are still capable of catching plenty of fish. They are very good for teaching children how to float-fish and can even give adults a lot of fun! The only thing you must watch out for is corrosion around the drag and spool casing. Give the reel a quick spray with WD40 after each trip and you should find that it will last you a couple of years or so, which is quite reasonable for a reel costing under £10. Then when it wears out you still have the rod, which you can match to a better reel, such as the Abumatic Bronco. It is a point worth bearing in mind because, although a lot of people turn their noses up at some of the cheaper gear on sale — and they are quite right to do so in the majority of cases — it does not always follow that every set is rubbish. Sometimes you can be quite agreeably surprised.

Centre Pins and Fly Reels
The last type of reel that I am going to mention is the centre pin. There are two types of centre pins — fly reels and 'trotting' centre pins, for lack of a better description — both of which have a large spool revolving inside an

The DAM Camaro LS45 is one of the better budget reels around at the time of writing.

open frame on a central pin. The handle is attached to the spool and the spool is regulated either directly by the thumb or through pressure applied internally when you engage a check. The primary difference between the two is the capacity of the spool. A fly reel is designed to take a very bulky line, so the spool is very deep. While this is excellent for fly-fishing, it almost totally precludes it from any other kind of fishing. If you loaded a fly reel with nylon monofilament and let it drift out with the current, you would find yourself winding-in for ages. Playing a fish could take hours and the chances are that it would have thrown the hook long before you managed to get it in. If you want to trot a light float with the current, perhaps for mullet or whiting, then you need a 'trotting' or 'match' centre pin. These have a very shallow spool, so that the line is wound on close to the rim. As the

spool has a very large diameter – say $4\frac{1}{2}$ in (115 mm) or more – then every full turn of the handle winds on some 14 in (approximately 35 cm) of line. You can play any fish properly and exercise great control over both your tackle and the fish that you expect to catch. The only problem is the limitation imposed on casting, which minimizes the opportunities for using centre pins in the sea. You can fly-fish for mackerel, bass or pollack, or you can trot a float for mullet, whiting or a few other species.

Now for fly reels. The huge demand for trout and salmon reels means there is a wide range to choose from; some, such as the Ryobi Sportsman, are very cheap while others are very expensive. It will probably pay you to start cheap and see if you like saltwater fly-fishing before spending a lot of money on tackle. If you want to start with something a little better then a reasonable compromise

The Ryobi 455 is typical of the fly reels that many people use for saltwater fly-fishing.

might be a reel such as the Ryobi 455, which I tested out earlier this year.

For trotting, however, there is no such huge range available. Some of the models that I have seen look as if they have been made by some unknown engineer turning them out in his garage for a bit of pocket money, with quality ranging from mediocre to diabolical. This means that you have to be careful if you decide to buy one because there are, quite frankly, some awful reels being offered for sale. I had a good look around because both my son and I are keen on mullet-fishing and we settled on two different centre pins from the Leeds group in Redditch. One was the Leeds reel, with the smaller $4\frac{1}{2}$ in (115 mm) diameter spool, and the other was the Match Reel with the $4\frac{3}{4}$ in (120 mm) spool. Both had a lovely smooth action and were ruggedly built without being over the top, balancing lightness with capacity and strength. Some of the other reels I saw were so heavy that they virtually belonged in the Stone Age!

* * *

Whichever reel you select, be it a multiplier or a centre pin, you will need to have a good general idea as to exactly when you can use them. To help you with that I will now discuss some suitable rods for the reels that I have mentioned and give you a rough idea as to exactly what you can use each outfit for. This will be covered in greater detail in subsequent chapters, but this section should help you to decide which of the outfits available might be the most entertaining or practical for the area that you are going to fish. It is also worth bearing in mind that there is a clear distinction between the two categories I just mentioned. On an entertainment basis there might be a short but extremely productive spell when you can use a particular combination. The fun you gain from those experiences may well justify your selection.

One example that 'springs' to mind is when the mackerel shoals move inshore in the early spring. On one of my marks we usually have an annual 3-week period when thousands of mackerel harry shoals of small fry against a slipway close to where I live. They go absolutely berserk and provide some spectacular sport. After catching many of them on spinners I decided to buy a 9 ft (2·74 m) fly rod with a cheap and cheerful reel, then see how the fish reacted to a tiny silver fly. The results were amazing! I can only get a few yards with it but frankly that is all that anyone needs. When a mackerel hits the fly the resulting fight is tremendous, providing such entertainment that it more than justifies, to me, the initial purchase of the outfit. On a practical basis another angler might look at this situation and decide that it is not worth spending any money on anything other than spinners. After all, if you want to be totally realistic, you may find that you can only use an outfit like this for perhaps half-a-dozen trips per year. It becomes a very subjective decision which can also be strongly influenced by your budget. You simply decide what suits you and stick with it.

RODS

Match Rods

One of the first rods that many light-tackle anglers experiment with are match rods. These are borrowed from the freshwater field — which, frankly, provides the basis for most decent light tackle — and are suitable for quite a wide variety of marks. They must, however, be matched with very light terminal rigs and their limitations borne strongly in mind. You can spin with them, especially if you use either an open face or a very small fixed spool, but you must bear in mind that the rings are small. This will limit the distance that you can cast and inflict more wear and tear on the line than do larger rings. They also tend to be unlined, which makes the problem worse. However, for float-fishing they are superb, especially if you match them with semi-weighted floats, such as Drennan Crystal Missiles. I have put one of these well beyond where I could see it and have caught lots of fish at much closer range. The resulting fights have been superb. The only caution that I would extend is that you select a mark where the currents are fairly light and where you have easy access to the water. You will need a landing net to net the fish, especially if you scale down the line to 2 or 3 lb (0·9 or 1·4 kg) breaking strain, and to carry out the netting you will need to be near the water. You will also need more or less flat-calm conditions. This tends to make match rods very popular in the summer but what people do not seem to realize is that they are just as effective in the winter for whiting, especially down steps on the outside of piers. The only addition you need is a Starlite taped to the top of the float. Add to this their superb handling of mullet, especially in the upper reaches of estuaries, and you can see that match rods make a very attractive proposition.

On a price basis you might find yourself agreeably surprised by the amount you have to pay. Obviously you can spend a great deal if you want to, but on the other hand you can get a reasonable rod very cheaply. I tried out a cheap and cheerful DAM rod — the Super-match — and found it handled the fish that I caught very well. If I needed distance I used it in conjunction with a light fixed spool — the CDi II 330 Match — but if I fished close in or trotted a float with a current then I used it with the Alvey Match centre pin. You might also like to look at some of the smaller open-face reels. I have had a great deal of fun with my Abumatic 1044 Syncro Match, which has proved ideal for float-fishing for pelagic species, but there are also quite a few others on the market which you might like to have a look at.

If you like a bit of do-it-yourself with regard to fishing, then why not look around boot sales until you find an old, somewhat tatty match rod. You can pick these up very cheaply and then take them home for a spot of renovation and alteration. Saw about 4 in (100 mm) off the top, which somewhat stiffens the action of the blank, then glue and whip on a lined $\frac{2}{5}$ in (10 mm) tip ring. Remove all wrappings from the handle and thread seven or eight sections of cork onto the blank. Push these up to where the first grip is going to be sited but do not glue them in place as of yet. Whip a Fuji snap-lock seat firmly into position and then glue the corks in place so that the first leg of the seat is covered by the corks. Make sure you have the distance right before you whip the seat in position. Simply take up the rod as if you are going to cast and position the seat where it is most comfortable for you. Thread another seven or eight cork sections for the second grip and then leave a gap before you put some more cork on the blank for the bottom grip. Once the glue is set, sand the cork lightly, making sure that you round the edges slightly as you do so. Sand all traces of gloss varnish from the handle.

Remove all the other rings and sand down the blank until it is back to its original colour with no traces of gloss varnish showing. Replace the smaller rings with no more than five intermediates ranging from $\frac{2}{5}$ in (10 mm) near the tip to 1 in (25 mm) placed about 3 ft (90 cm) up the blank from the reel seat. Use the same colour whipping thread as you used for the reel seat and site the other rings so that they are staggered in order of decreasing size, with the smallest space between the tip ring and first intermediate, and the largest space between the butt ring and the next. The distance between each ring will then decrease slightly so that the rings, when you sight down the rod, will create a tunnel effect, with each ring neatly framed by its predecessor. You will have to work out actual distances from the length of the blank exposed after you have completed the handle.

Once you have finished this part of your alterations then use a good-quality rod finish to give all the whippings and the blank a nice veneer of gloss. Leave it 24 hours and then put on a second coat. Depending on the finish you use you might have to give it a third coat a day later. Leave it to dry thoroughly and when you have finished you will find that you

WHIPPING A RING TO A BLANK

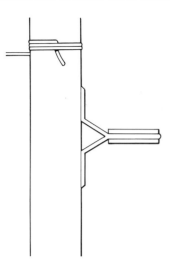

(1) Secure one side of the ring to the blank with masking tape and begin the opposite whipping, trapping the end of the thread beneath itself.

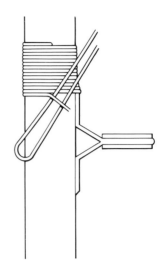

(2) Coil the thread around the blank and the end of the thread, to within $\frac{1}{5}$ in (5 mm) of the stopping point, by rotating the blank. Lay a nylon loop along the blank and continue whipping over this.

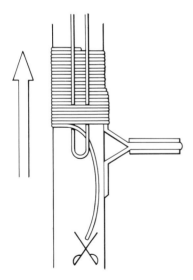

(3) Finish whipping and cut the thread, leaving an end of about 4 in (10 cm). Thread the end through the nylon loop and pull it through the whipping using the loop.

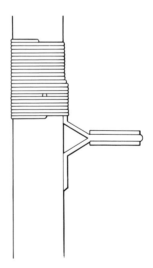

(4) Pull tight, using the spare end, and trim.

have a lovely light rod which is ideal for spinning and float-fishing. You will be able to cast a long way with light tackle and have a really good fight from each fish.

If you have never done a whipping before, please do not be put off. With a little practice you will soon find yourself making a very professional job. They are not really that difficult, the main ingredients for successful whippings being correct tension and patience. It also helps, if you are attaching a ring, to start on the rod blank and progress upwards to the legs of the ring. If you start on the ring and go down you may find that the thread slips from the leg, resulting in an untidy job, although this can be ameliorated by lightly filing the leg so that it tapers nicely to the blank. If you follow the instructions below carefully and refer to the diagrams on page 25 then you should not go far wrong.

The first step is to secure the ring before you whip it. Use masking tape for this, checking that the ring is perfectly in line with the tip ring and then taping the opposite side to the leg that you are going to whip to the blank. Put a turn of whipping thread around the blank a little way down from the leg that you are going to whip, trapping the end of the thread beneath itself. Rotate the blank while holding the thread so that it coils around both the blank and the end of the thread, securing it tightly in position. Continue coiling the thread by rotating the blank. This will soon cover most of the leg until you reach a point approximately $\frac{1}{5}$ in (5 mm) from where you will have to stop. Lay a nylon loop next to the blank with the eye of the loop resting at the side of the ring. Continue to whip until you cannot go any further, then cut the thread about 4 in (100 mm) from the final coil and thread this spare end through the nylon loop. Pull on the opposite end of the loop, holding both ends tightly, and it will slide from underneath the whipping, bringing the end of the thread with it. Pull tight – carefully – with the end and then trim it next to the whipping. Remove the masking tape from the other leg

and then repeat the whole operation.

Once you have done this a couple of times you will soon find yourself doing some very good whippings. The main thing is not to rush and to be prepared to take back any coils that start to go wrong. Have a look at the diagrams, take it step by step and eventually you should find yourself with a superb little rod. At that point why not customize it with a silver or gold signwriting pen? With a little care you can make a really attractive result. If you are anything like me it will also give you a great deal of pleasure to catch a fish on tackle that you have made yourself.

Legering Rods

If you do not have the time or inclination to build a rod such as this then a useful compromise is to investigate freshwater legering rods. These are somewhat sturdier than the match rods but still extremely light by comparison with regular saltwater tackle. They tend to have larger rings than match models and accordingly lend themselves very nicely to both spinning and light float-fishing. I regularly use mine with the smallest of the West Country sliding floats, which are really too heavy for match rods but are ideal on the heavier legers. Compared to other sea floats they are very much smaller and consequently that much more sensitive for bite detection. Used with legering rods they can be cast up to 70 yd (65 m) from the shore, which makes them ideal for long-distance floating for mackerel, garfish, scad and pollack.

With regard to spinning you will usually find that they will handle spinners weighing up to $1\frac{1}{4}$ oz (35 g) quite easily, which again makes them ideal for the species I have just mentioned. One of my favourites is the 1 oz (28 g) Cebar, which closely resembles the old German sprats. A legering rod will cast one of these nearly 100 yd (90 m) and will give an incredible fight when you hook a decent fish. The only thing you need do is to make sure that the drag on your reel is set to allow any bigger fish to run, especially if you scale your line down as light as you can go. Personally I like to use an open-face reel matched with 4–6 lb (1·8–2·7 kg) breaking-strain line for spinning and 8 lb (3·6 kg) breaking-strain line for float-fishing. I find the heavier line helps to absorb the shock of casting and consequently minimizes tackle losses. Some of my friends find smaller fixed spools easier to use, but one tip we all use is to tape the reel in position with PVC tape before we slide the coasters over the feet of the reel. This locks the reel in position, which is important because you can get a lot of stress on both the rod and reel during a decent fight. Without the tape the reel tends to migrate out of line with the rings and I have even seen a reel fall off on the cast following a particularly hard struggle. Using tape will cut out that problem, although another solution is permanently to attach a Fuji snap-lock seat to the handle of the rod.

With regard to actual models there is a wide range available, but you need to make sure that the rings are not too small. They should also be lined. One I particularly liked was the Ryobi John Wilson Specialist, which handled float and spinning well, but also doubled up with a swing tip when I wanted to use a swimfeeder on a simple leger rig for mullet. The swimfeeder — which is a small container into which you can pack groundbait or samples of the bait that you are offering — replaces the lead and is cast into a likely spot, such as a little way out past the outfall from a sewer. The samples, perhaps maggots, escape from the holes in the swimfeeder and attract the mullet closer until they find your hookbait. It is a good tactic, although you will need a strong stomach to handle both the smell and some of the items you will need to remove from your line! The swing tip, which is screwed into the top eye of the rod, then helps to highlight any bites so that you end up with a higher ratio of hooked fish to bites.

Fly Rods
Fly-fishing may appear to be somewhat of a specialist approach, but it can nonetheless be used to catch a variety of sea fish, including mackerel, bass, pollack, herring and garfish. One of the main points to bear in mind is that you will need control and distance, with the length of the fly rod influenced by the marks that you intend to fish. Personally I would go for a fly rod between 10 and 11 ft (3 and 3·4 m) in length for most locations, but in some you may have to scale down to 9 ft (2·74 m). You will also have to be careful of bystanders!

If you have never used a fly rod before, it may feel a bit odd reeling-in with the reel at the very bottom of the rod. I used to find this a bit awkward but eventually ended up getting a fly rod — from the Ryobi Challenge series — with an extension that fitted into the bottom of the blank. This made it a lot easier to handle.

Carp Rods
If your budget or environment restricts you to one rod for light-tackle usage, then the best choice you could probably make would be a carp rod. These have the versatility and power to handle most light-tackle applications around the country, while also being comfortable to hold and pleasant to use. They react well to a fighting fish and can cast either leger or float a very long way. Matched with a multiplier or fixed spool they can cast a 2 oz (57 g) lead weight up to 100 yd (90 m) out — which is ample for piers, estuaries and the majority of headlands — and are so sensitive that your bite detection is considerably enhanced. Whether you are after flounders, bass, mackerel or dogfish, to name but a few of the species which you can go after with a carp rod, you will find that the right rod will add new dimensions to your enjoyment of the sport.

When you come to look at carp rods you will find that there are many models available, each of which is graded according to the strength of the blank. Generally, these range from a 1¼ lb (0·6 kg) test curve up to 2½ lb (1·1 kg). As a broad rule of thumb I would suggest that the lighter blanks are ideal for floating, mulleting, spinning and using medium plugs after bass, while the heavier rods handle medium-sized floats, spinning, wrassing, large plugs and legering. Basically the heavier rods can do all that the lighter ones can, although there is a slight loss in sensitivity. It therefore makes sense to use them where the currents are a bit stronger or where you expect the fish to be bigger. On the other hand you may be more interested in float-fishing and want the rod to double-up for mullet, in which case it will pay you to stick to the lighter blanks. It is entirely up to you. See which interests you most and make your own decision accordingly.

I looked at quite a few carp rods when I started writing this book and decided that the best way to test them out was to get in a few models and give them a really good work-out to see how they performed. Quite a lot of people helped me with this, especially the youngsters from the Torbay Association of Sea Anglers, so that we managed not only to give the rods a thorough pasting but also to catch a considerable number of fish. After a season's active use they had all taken and, quite frankly, shrugged off an awful lot of use. They performed very well. I will list the models we tested according to the companies that produced them:

DAM 2378 330 Prima Carp and 2393 334 Fighter Carp (budget).

Ryobi 12 ft (3·7 m) Super Specialist.

Normark Nova Carp and Pro-Specialist Carp.

All of these models are based on blanks of 11 ft (3·4 m) or more but, besides conventional carp rods, there are also stalking rods which are much shorter, mostly under 9 ft (2·74 m) long. When we tested these we found them to be ideal for floating, light legering or spinning in areas where there were obstructions which made casting difficult or almost impossible with longer rods, as is the case with many

piers. They performed very well. We also used them on headlands and found them to be ideal for chasing bass from our boat. I think it is also worth mentioning that the two models we tested, in the hands of children aged under 10 years, won five competitions, including an open Junior Championship, the under-11 section of another Junior open and two club competitions in which they fished against adult entrants. Although the two models – the DAM Andy Little Stalking and the Ryobi John Wilson Wanderer – were shorter than the conventional carp rods they still cast well and gave very enjoyable fights.

Pike Rods

If you are into bass-fishing, you will know that much of the time you will be fishing from beaches or at the mouths of estuaries, sometimes into the face of some pretty stiff surf. On occasion it will pay you to step up to a 3 oz (85 g) weight, which is a bit too heavy for the carp rods. A 3 lb (1·4 kg) test-curve pike rod, especially if it is matched with a multiplier, will handle this size of weight and put it 100 yd (90 m) out if it is needed. It is also the next step down from a beachcaster on many other marks, where the weight will hold in the current – as long as you use a breakaway quick-release lead – and proceed to catch flatfish or other demersal species. They are ideal for legering from piers and very useful for reaching fish that lie in the band from 80–100 yd (75–90 m) out.

There are not as many pike rods on the market as there are carp rods – probably because freshwater anglers double up their carp rods for pike – but there are a few available. I tested the DAM Prima 'Big fish Pike' and found it did very well. It may not have the range of a high-power beachcaster, but it certainly matched the casts of a lot of people who thought they were casting much further than they actually were. This is one point which is worth bearing in mind. Many people have highly exaggerated notions of how far they are casting. If you have ever gone to a casting event and actually paced the distance that you cast, then you will quickly realize that most people, despite a load of codswallop about casting 150 yd (135 m) or more, will actually be lucky if they can cast 100 yd (90 m). Add the air resistance from the bait and they are probably down to 80 yd (75 m). If you can cast 125 yd (115 m) with bait then you are doing very well, so do not be put off by comments from other anglers.

I experienced a similar situation about a fortnight ago. One angler repeatedly insisted that a 150 yd (135 m) cast was necessary to put you on the sand at a particular mark. He then performed his 'long-distance cast' to demonstrate just how far that was. Although he tried hard, the rod was overmatched by the size of lead he was using and this, coupled with poor casting technique, drastically cut down the distance that he might have been able to cast. The lead was in the air for under 4 seconds and came down about 60 yd (55 m) out. 'There you are!' he said. '150 yards, just what you need to get on the sand!' Now I had no interest in disillusioning him, but it just goes to show that there are many locations which people *think* you cannot reach with light tackle, when the chances are that you probably can. The only sure way to find out if you can reach the hot spot at a particular mark is to try it and see for yourself!

Bass Rods

Much of what I said about pike rods is equally true about bass rods, although there is an extra point to bear in mind. Many companies seem to hold some very strange ideas about what actually suits sea-anglers and have produced some very peculiar models. You will notice, for example, that although this is a book on light tackle, there is no section on the 'mullet rods' which some companies produce. That is because the supposedly specialist mullet rods that I have seen tend to be so uniformly awful that I will not give them the space. They are generally crude and insensitive models which have combined the worst of both sea- and coarse-fishing. I have yet to find one that I would even consider buying, while most of them should have been aborted at the design stage and completely reworked.

You have much the same situation, though to a lesser degree, with bass rods. The only one I tried and liked was the DAM Carbomesh Bass, which I matched to the CDFS free-spool fixed spool. It has never let me down and is now, quite frankly, my favourite rod for legering from piers. It is also sufficiently versatile to use for legering from rocky headlands, where the rocks give way to sand, on beaches after bass and also up estuaries, even where I need a bit of distance. It will put a baited line out 100 yd (90 m) and yet is still light enough to enable me to get a most enjoyable fight from the fish that I catch. A prime example is one of my local piers, where a number of people fish regularly for dogfish. A 2 lb (0·9 kg) fish puts up such a spirited performance that many people have been fooled into thinking that I have caught something bigger. When they have caught fish their beachcasters have certainly bent over, but it is only because they have been reeling-in so quickly that the fish has become a dead weight in the water. On my rod the fish, be it a dogfish or a bass, has an opportunity to fight which, for me, epitomizes the difference between fishing and angling.

Baitcasters

These are probably the most overlooked rods that you are ever likely to encounter. Basically they are a light spinning blank which is run into a trigger-grip reel seat. They are sometimes fitted with a pistol grip and at other times have a small extension which you can balance down your forearm. They are superb for light-tackle usage and, if you match them with a small baitcasting multiplier, can provide some of the most exciting sport that you are ever going to have.

Frankly I do not know why people have not clicked onto just how good these rods can be. I think it is largely because they are so completely different from beachcasters or any of the other rods that you see people using. This is a great pity as the rods weigh only a few ounces, which means that you cast them single-handed and obtain terrific fun from any fish that you catch. Match them with a closed-face reel and you get long, silky-smooth casts with virtually no tangles. You also have terrific control over the lure so that you can guide it in such a way that it becomes far more attractive to the fish that you are after. Baitfish do, after all, make sudden turns and dives in a fairly confined pathway through the water. With a baitcaster you can imitate those movements. The presentation of the lure is fairly realistic and consequently more appealing than the bionic lunges which are imparted if you attempt the same thing with a longer rod.

If you want to float-fish, you will find that a small multiplier will give the rod the ability to make long, smooth casts, whilst handling any fish with a degree of sensitivity very few outfits can match. The same is true if you are drifting or legering from a boat close inshore. Even the smallest fish will put a deceptive bend in the rod. Get a bass or a decent wrasse and it feels as if a shark has just swallowed your bait!

Baitcasters can offer some of the most exciting sport available to the British angler and yet, despite this, they are extremely difficult to obtain. ABU bring a few rods into the UK every year, with some particularly good ones among them, but on the whole there are very few to choose from, especially good ones where the blank has the power to deal with any bigger fish that chance along. There are some cheaper ones on the market, which can be very exciting to use for the smaller pelagic species, such as mackerel, scad or garfish, but if you want to get a better one then you really have to shop around and even be prepared to order specially from your local tackle shop. The tragedy is that they are not even particularly expensive! I bought a superb model for £25 and found it so good that I went back for two more for my children. It really is ludicrous and I find it hard to believe

that British anglers — as one representative put it — are so unimaginative that they are not prepared to try anything even the slightest bit out of the ordinary. I hope you prove him wrong. Baitcasters are a lot of fun and, with the size of the fish that we are catching going down every year, it is certainly time that we seized any opportunity to increase the quality of our sport. Baitcasters are one way of doing just that.

Spinning Rods

There are many, many spinning rods to choose from, most of which have, unfortunately, been misnamed. Every year thousands of rods are sold to people who are only interested in catching a few fish when they go on holiday or who just want to drop a line off the pier every now and again. Often these people expect their rod to do a little bit of everything, so the manufacturers oblige by putting on enormous rings and building into their rods sufficient strength to take any little knocks that occur along the way. Now there is nothing wrong with that but this 'Jack of all trades' approach does *not* make the rod a spinning rod. What it really makes is a holiday or a beginner's rod. Unfortunately my guess would be that if the manufacturers termed these 'holiday rods' then their sales would drop considerably. I suspect that people who might buy them as spinning rods would turn their noses up at starter rods. I get the impression that the manufacturers think pretty much the same thing, so the term 'spinning rods' is unnecessarily widened to cover the holiday as well as the specialist market.

If you decide to invest in a spinning rod — and a good one can be a pleasure to use — then a broad rule of thumb might be to look at the price first of all. If you want quality, then be prepared to pay for it. If you pay out £20 for a rod, then it would be unrealistic to expect it to give you the same performance as a quality model. A good spinning rod is slim, resilient, with a steely feel to it that compresses during the cast and then delivers that extra punch to the spinner as it flicks it out to sea. Unlike many of the rods offered for sale as spinning rods they are lightweight but sufficiently powerful to put effective side-strain on any bass or bigger fish that comes along. They will cast a float or spinner a very long way and drive the hook firmly home upon the strike. Now those specifications mean that you will not be able to get a very good one very cheaply. Like everything else you get what you pay for.

When you do look around, you will still find that there are some very nice rods being offered for sale. The Normark Conquest is a good example, for although the 10 ft (3 m) model retails at over £60, it is a delight to use, casting a 1 oz (28 g) spinner a very long way. It is typical of how a good-quality spinning rod ought to be designed.

Poles

I am not going to delve into poles in any great detail in this section because Chapter 3 is devoted entirely to pole-fishing. However, put very briefly, poles are essentially an extended fishing rod where the reel has been replaced with a length of elastic to help absorb the sudden lunges of any fish that are hooked. They are very effective for species that come close to the shore and are both lightweight and easy to handle, although you do need more or less flat-calm conditions to get the best out of them. If you live near a headland or a pier where you can get right down to the water then you will find that they can be really exciting to use, especially in the summer when there are considerably more fish within their range than many anglers might suppose. They are not children's toys but are indeed a fascinating and enjoyable way to fish. I have seen my children outfish conventional tackle on them time and again! As to price, well, quite frankly there is no need for anything really expensive for sea-fishing and some very good sport is available on telescopics retailing at under £20. If you really get into pole-fishing then you can always go for something better

but to start off with I would suggest that you get something cheap and see if you like it. If you do, you will soon find that there is a considerable range on sale, with coarse anglers purchasing models retailing well in excess of £1,000. I certainly would not go to those lengths but I am sure you will be able to suit both your taste and your pocket if you shop around.

LINE, TACKLE AND ACCESSORIES

Once you have decided on an outfit then you will need to get hold of some line and make a selection of terminal tackle. There are some very interesting developments going on in the field of fishing lines, but what you really need is a line which is supple and resistant to kinks, has a high knot-strength and is resistant to abrasion. Diameter should be fairly fine but be careful of lines which have been pre-stretched. Some brands are very prone to snapping upon sudden impact, which can make crack-offs fairly common and also creates difficulties if a fish suddenly turns and lunges in a different direction. You should also be wary of claims regarding the near-invisibility of certain lines. A tangle means that the mess is going to be awfully hard to clear up, especially if you cannot see what you are doing. With the exception of mulleting I prefer a high-visibility line, such as Stren, or supple lines, such as Toray from Normark or Damyl Megalon. I know some anglers claim that fish are put off by brightly coloured lines but frankly, while that may apply to coarse-fishing, it certainly does not to sea-fishing. If that were the case, the longliners would never catch anything! I have also seen plenty of fish — including an 8 lb (3·6 kg) bass — caught on handlines made with bright orange cordolene. Considering the cuttyhunk nature of its diameter I really would not worry too much about a fine golden line. I do not think its colour makes an ounce of difference to the fish, but it will certainly help you to sort out any tangles.

While on the subject of lines there is a development which I have been watching with a fair degree of apprehension. That development is the manufacture of aramid lines which contain a fair degree of kevlar. These lines offer a very high strength-to-diameter ratio, making them much thinner than nylon monofilament. Some of the prototypes that are currently around are certainly impressive, with 70 lb (31·8 kg) breaking-strain aramid the same diameter as 18 lb (8·2 kg) monofilament. Now that sounds most advantageous and, if everything else was in order, could revolutionize the reels that we use. Unfortunately the line is not merely strong, it is resistant to sunlight and all the other factors which adversely affect monofilament. Good news in some ways but not when you realize that the line is non-biodegradable. You break a length off in the water — and we all do from time to time — and it sits there, year in, year out, gradually turning our inshore marks into such a trailing mass of snags that they could well become unfishable. Personally this is one development which I would like to see investigated a lot further before it comes onto the market properly. At the moment, fortunately, it is very expensive, which will limit the demand, but I do hope that the manufacturers will take the time and trouble to ensure that they build some sort of safeguard into the line to prevent it ever becoming a problem around our coast. Until they do, I, for one, will totally boycott its use.

With regard to terminal tackle there are several items which you will need and many which you will not need. Tackle shops offer a bewildering selection of knick-knacks, many of which are totally unnecessary. The essential items obviously depend on the fish that you intend to go for but, on a general basis, you will need floats and matching weights, breakaway or Aquapedo leads, both 2 and 3 oz (57 and 85 g), 1 oz (28 g) Arlesey Bombs, swivels, two spools of trace, one heavier than your main line and one weaker, hooks in various patterns, easy links and beads. If you get into spinning, you might like to add a few plugs and spinners and if you get into mulleting you

might like to add a couple of swimfeeders or non-toxic lead weights. If you are interested in float-fishing, it is also a good idea to include a spool of red power gum for the tying of stop knots.

There are two other items which I would strongly recommend that you buy, namely a tackle box and a landing net. With regard to tackle boxes, what you select will depend on what type of fishing you intend to do and where you intend to do it. If you are climbing down cliffs, I would strongly recommend a waistcoat-style of carrier, such as the Ryobi Wanderer. This has pockets which are big enough to take smaller boxes for endgear, torches and even a vacuum flask. It will leave your hands fairly unencumbered for climbing and can also be used to distribute the weight of your tackle in a comfortable manner. If you get into spinning, then you might prefer a more conventional tackle box, so that all your gear is laid out for you to see at a glance. The only problem nowadays is that some of the best lures are made of a latex containing built-in inhibitors to prevent them becoming hard and cracking-up. These inhibitors are pretty strong and can, in fact, eat their way right through some plastics, making it important that you get a tackle box which is labelled 'worm-proof', a term we borrowed from the USA. There are quite a few good ones around, but two I particularly liked were the Plano 1232 Tackle Racker and the Plano 6303 Tackle Box. Both are very good boxes, although the Tackle Racker has the edge as far as its storage capacity and division of bits and pieces is concerned.

Landing nets are another essential if you are going to use light tackle. You cannot depend on swinging a fish out of the water, as most people seem to do with anything they catch on a beachcaster. You might be able to do this with a very small fish but, if you catch anything decent, you will really need a landing net close to hand. There are quite a few around but whichever you choose I would recommend that you pay attention to two

The Plano 6303 Tackle Box (left) and the 1232 Tackle Racker.

particular points. The first is the length of the handle. Play it safe and get a telescopic one, preferably one which extends to 8 or 9 ft (2·4 or 2·74 m). On many marks a shorter one may be fine at high tide but once the tide goes out you will be glad of the extra length. The other consideration is the mesh. If you use knotless mesh this is much kinder to the epidermis of any fish that you catch, removing far fewer scales than other nets. If you intend to put the fish back, this is a serious consideration. The less damage the better because the epidermis is there to protect the fish from infection, some parasites and fungal complaints. It will also pay you to get a bigger rather than a smaller net. It may look ridiculous netting a mackerel, but on the day you catch a 10 lb (4·5 kg) bass it will look just the right size!

CHAPTER THREE

A FUN WAY TO BEGIN

People smiled indulgently as Becky swung her pole to the side, carefully choosing the point where the rocks gave way into deeper water. I heard one of them say: 'It's a bit better than a handline!' and then he laughed, smiling at the look of concentration on my daughter's face. Becky glanced up for a moment, slightly offended, but then turned back to watch her float. Already it was bobbing, jittering about on the surface of the water before abruptly being drawn into the depths.

Her reaction was immediate: she struck straight away to set the hook, then lifted the pole as high as she could. The reaction of the wrasse was just as predictable: it dived for the rocks and then turned and ran against the pressure from above. Becky turned the pole away from the direction in which it was

Pole-fishing is great fun for both adults and children.

running, then used the extra length to steer the fish away from the weeds and out into clearer water.

The elastic link from the tip of the pole to the tackle was alarmingly stretched, but each time the fish ran it seemed to stretch just that little bit less than the time before. Gradually the fish tired until it was drawn, unresisting, to the waiting net. It was not a huge fish, probably about $1\frac{1}{4}$ lb (0.6 kg) in weight, but the fight it put up was terrific.

The angler who had spoken earlier wandered over to have a look. He nodded as he saw the ease with which the barbless hook was removed, then raised an eyebrow in surprise as I slipped it into the keepnet we had positioned for the fish that were caught. Becky hesitated for a moment, deciding whether to use prawns or ragworm for bait, then quickly put on a prawn and dropped it a bit further out. She had longer to wait this time, several minutes passing before her float was drawn slowly downwards, stopped for a second and then carried on as before. Once again she swept the pole aloft, but this time the fish turned and ran straight away, lunging to first one side then the other before it tired sufficiently for her to get it in the net. Then, as she brought it ashore, we were able to see what it was: a nice pollack, at least for this area, weighing just under 2 lb (0.9 kg).

Over the next half-hour both Becky and Anthony took several wrasse and pollack on their 16 ft 4 in (5 m) poles. Then Anthony shouted for the net. I didn't pay too much attention at first, Anthony having a tendency to exaggerate, but that changed as soon as I had a good look at what he was doing. The end of the pole was under the water while Anthony was straining to try and keep the fish up and away from the weeds it was so desperately trying to reach. He succeeded, but the fish still turned and fought for several minutes more before we could finally get it to head towards the net. It didn't like the look of that so it turned and dived one final time before it was once again brought to the

surface. This time we were able to land it, a nice wrasse weighing just over $3\frac{1}{2}$ lb (1.6 kg).

The other angler wandered over, then grinned as we lifted the keepnet and released a stream of over 30 wrasse and pollack into the water. 'Excuse me,' he said, a bit sheepishly as he had only caught a solitary garfish while the children were enjoying much better sport. 'That's a pole, isn't it? Are they very expensive?'

I heard a little sound behind me and could not help grinning at the smug expression on Becky's face. 'It's a lot better than a handline,' she said with some relish, then passed him a pole which she had just baited with a prawn. The wrasse were, as before, obliging. His question was, however, a good one because poles can range in price from under £10 to well over £1,000, depending on both the

Becky had some fun on the pole with these fish.

The result of just over an hour's fishing on the pole: about 30 lb (13.6 kg) of assorted wrasse, pollack and mackerel.

model and what you want to do with it. If you go coarse-fishing as well as sea-fishing, it might well be worthwhile investing in one a little better. However, speaking from a purely personal point of view, I think there is very little to be gained from the purchase of an expensive pole intended purely for sea-fishing. Frankly, I think you would probably find that most of the cheaper telescopics on the market are perfectly adequate for the majority of the fish that you are likely to encounter. For example, on 13 ft and 16 ft 4 in (4 and 5 m) telescopics my children and I have taken wrasse, pout, whiting, red bream, bass and pollack, while on the 19 ft 8 in (6 m) pole we have also taken mackerel, garfish and flounders. We have caught plenty of fish, even though our most expensive pole cost less than £20! The cheapest was a Silstar 13 ft (4 m) telescopic which we purchased for £8·99, while the most expensive was a DAM 19 ft 8 in (6 m) Stippi retailing, at the time of writing, at only £17·99. You might say that they are cheap and cheerful, but for all that they do the job and they do it very well. Why spend more than you need to?

If you do decide to buy a pole, how you rig it up will depend on the area that you want to fish. However, before you do, you must adapt it for sea-fishing. There are two ways of doing this and these are shown in the diagrams on page 38. The first is to buy a PTFE external bush and rig the pole with internal elastic secured to a bung, while the second is to use elastic links attached to the eye at the tip of the pole.

Although a pole set up with internal elastic has a very nice feel to it, you use a lot more elastic than if you are going to use a link. This translates into extra stretch, which gives species such as wrasse a very good chance of reaching cover and snagging your tackle. Then, if the elastic breaks, it can be very fiddly trying to re-thread a replacement. Add to this the fact that you will probably have to saw a few inches off the tip of the pole to secure a good fit for the bush and you can see that

internal elastic has its problems. That said, for species such as flounders, mackerel and garfish, which run rather than try to reach cover, internal elastic is definitely superior to links. The main reason for this is that the extra 'spring' of the 19 ft 8 in (6 m) pole can lead to links tangling around the end, which can become irritating. Consequently I use internal elastic for poles that are 19 ft 8 in (6 m) or over in length, while reserving elastic links for poles of 16 ft 4 in (5 m) and under.

Setting up an internal elastic is something better done at home rather than down by the shore. Unscrew the butt cap from the bottom of the pole and remove the top section. Measure the tip diameter and then glue the PTFE bush into the position where you can get the tightest fit, cutting off a small piece of the blank if you have to. Use a hot-melt glue so that you can remove the bush if you ever need to replace it, putting the glue on the pole and then sliding the bush over the top. Make sure that it is secure. If it is at all loose then the chances are that it will come off at the most inconvenient time, probably when you are in the middle of playing a fish! If it does not feel safe, just take it off and cut a little extra off the blank until you do get a really tight fit.

The next thing you need to do is to find an appropriate diameter plug to fit inside the base of the tip section. Commercial ones are available, but they may have to be trimmed to fit the pole. On these plugs, or 'bungs' as some people call them, there are both the discs that will plug the blank and some holes into which the elastic will be tied. Leave a hole both above and below the disc that you choose, then cut off the surplus. To the bottom hole you will need to tie a short length of nylon. This will enable you to pull the plug out of the blank if you ever need to thread a replacement piece of elastic, which will, in turn, be tied to the hole above the disc.

Once you have done this most of the hard work is over. With luck many years will pass before you have to replace either bung or PTFE bush. One thing you will have to do,

RIGGING A POLE

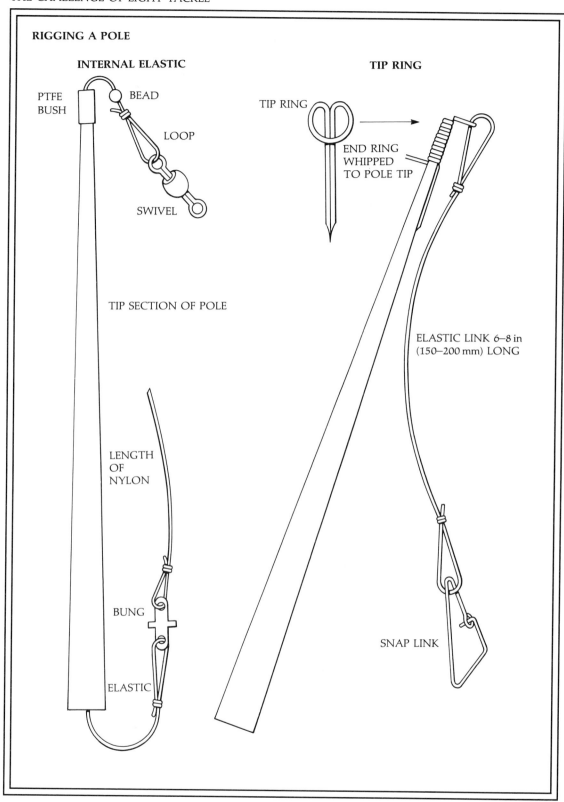

INTERNAL ELASTIC

PTFE
BUSH

BEAD

LOOP

SWIVEL

TIP SECTION OF POLE

LENGTH
OF
NYLON

BUNG

ELASTIC

TIP RING

TIP RING

END RING
WHIPPED
TO POLE TIP

ELASTIC LINK 6–8 in
(150–200 mm) LONG

SNAP LINK

however, is to replace broken elastic, although you can keep this to a minimum by using grade 8 (super) pole elastic. This breaks at over 10 lb (4·5 kg), which is far more pressure than the pole can exert, so if you use no more than 8 lb (3·6 kg) breaking-strain monofilament for the actual tackle, you will find that the elastic will usually only break after a lot of use, when it has become rather worn.

You will also find that threading a pole can be simplified if you make a threading tool to help you. Simply take a piece of 30 lb (13·6 kg) line, which is stiff enough to be threaded through the tip by hand, and pass it through the bush and down the tip section until it protrudes at least 1 ft (30 cm) from the bottom. Superglue a length of 10 lb (4·5 kg) line (you cannot use a knot, it will not go through the bush) to the stronger line and pull this down the blank until it too is protruding from the bottom with at least 1 ft (30 cm) left showing at the top. Make sure the glue is thoroughly dry before you pull the line through the bush. The last thing you want to do is to block it up with a bit of superglued nylon! Tie a loop to the bit sticking out of the tip and pass the elastic through the loop. Double the elastic back so that the 'spare end' is at least 1 ft (30 cm) long, then pull on the other end of the nylon. As the loop passes through the bush, so it will bring the elastic with it.

Use a loop knot to attach the elastic to the top hole of the bung and then plug the base of the tip section. Slide a bead onto the elastic at the tip and then stretch it to tie a loop knot. Don't stretch it too far, but certainly pull it sufficiently tightly for the loop to nestle against the bush the moment that you release it. The bead prevents the elastic from slipping through the bush and the loop left showing is a convenient place to put on a snap link. This will be used to attach whatever tackle you are going to fish with. If you like, you can get rid of the snap link by sliding a swivel onto the elastic so that it is trapped on the loop, tying your tackle direct to the swivel. This is probably stronger, the only problem being that,

every time you cut it free, you decrease the depth at which you can fish. If you are setting up new tackle every time this will not be a problem, but if you want to use tackles that you have made up in advance, then you will only be able to use them a couple of times before they start to become too short to use. Personally I like to have a range of tackles ready to be clipped straight to the tip of the rod. I store them on pole-winders and use them time and again. The swivel does, however, provide an alternative for people who do not like clips. If they wish they can always use loop knots and split rings instead.

If your pole is less than 19 ft 8 in (6 m) long, then it will probably be best to use external links rather than internal elastic. These elastic links are easier to make up and can be clipped straight onto the eye at the tip of the pole. Unfortunately, these eyes are not very robust and need either reinforcing with a piece of sturdy nylon whipped and superglued tightly to the blank, or replacing altogether. I personally prefer the latter option. You can make a very strong tip ring quite simply out of stainless wire just by folding a piece back on itself to the length you desire and then turning down the fold to make an eye. Taper the ends of the wire with judicious filing or grinding. This can be glued and whipped to the blank. The tapered wire ends will help you achieve a neat whipping while the ring itself should be strong enough to give you many years of active service.

Once you have sorted out the eye, the rest is simplicity itself. Attach a snap link to the eye and than take a piece of either elastic or white power gum some 8–9 in (200–250 mm) long. Which you use is up to you, the main difference being that power gum will not stretch as far as elastic. It does, however, last a lot longer and still stretches well enough to do the job. Tie a loop in one end and clip this to the eye. Slide on a swivel and then tie a second loop so that the swivel is free-sliding on the loop. Your tackle will be tied to the swivel and, when you finish fishing, the elastic link

BLOOD KNOT

(1) Push the line through the eye and double it back.

(2) Twist the spare end around the main line seven times.

(3) Take the spare end through the loop next to the eye.

(4) Pull tight and trim.

can be unclipped from the pole and wound on the pole-winder along with your gear.

Once you have rigged up your pole, you need to decide both where you are going to fish and what tackle to use. There are really only three options for this: free-lining, where the only tackle is a hook on a long piece of nylon; float-fishing, with the smallest floats you can get away with; or legering. These are all simple tackles, but you will need to make sure that your knots are well tied and secure. Most anglers use blood knots, which are all right as long as you tie them properly, but a growing number are also starting to use variations on the grinner knot, especially in relation to hooks. The reason for this is that the blood knot, when it is completed, has a nylon spur which sticks out at 90 degrees to the knot. Purists argue that this can jab a fish when it takes the bait, scaring it into spitting it out quickly and so reducing the amount of time available for striking. By contrast the grinner lays the trimmed end along the line that you are using for the trace. It is less likely to jab the fish and so gives you a fraction longer to strike.

To tie a blood knot you start by threading the line through the eye of the hook and pulling through a few inches to give you something to work with. Twist the end around the main line seven times and then tuck the end through the loop nearest to the eye of the swivel. Lubricate the knot with a bit of saliva and then pull the knot tight. Trim the end and you are finished. These stages are shown in the diagrams on page 40.

The grinner knot starts in much the same way. Pull a few inches — say about 6 in (150 mm) — through the eye of the hook and then twist it four times around the main line. Put the end through the loop nearest the eye of the hook — making sure that you pass it through from above — and pull most of the end through so that it forms a much bigger loop. Pass the line through this bigger loop — once again from above — and then coil it three times around the twisted strands. Lubricate

and pull the spare end first of all so that it rises as far as it can away from the hook. Wet the knot again and then pull on the main line to fully tighten the knot. Finish off by trimming the spare end. The result should be a small and very neat knot. The diagrams on page 42 should help, but if you do not get it right the first time just be patient and go back and try again. It will not take you long to master, but will prove very useful if you decide to go free-lining for predators.

Free-lining is a useful tactic for bass, garfish and pollack, although by its nature it is limited to either rocky headlands, where there is plenty of cover and a good depth of water close in, or places such as steps on piers, slipways, etc. It seems to be most successful on early-morning sessions where there is little noise or movement to disturb the fish. Simply tie on a hook to a piece of nylon the same length as your pole, bait it with a small livebait and lower it into the water. You must then wait for a bite. This can obviously take a while so it sometimes pays to have a system for holding the pole worked out in advance. I use a seat box which has been fitted with a Taper Trak from MPH Associates. Essentially the Taper Trak is a pole or rod rest which bolts to the side of your tackle box. You can adjust it to suit your individual requirements and simply remove the arms when you put the box away. It is a simple and robust system which is good for both poles and conventional rods.

If you are trying for bass, please bear in mind that they will often come very close to the shore. On rocky headlands I have taken many that were less than 3 ft (90 cm) away from the rocks. It may seem odd just dropping your bait at your feet, but it often pays dividends. You will need to be as quiet and as still as possible to make the best of this tactic. Bass can be very cautious, especially when there is little background movement or noise to disguise your activity, so a loud or sudden noise may easily drive them away. If they are easily spooked then borrow a leaf from the

VARIATION ON A GRINNER KNOT

(1) Pull about 6 in (150 mm) of line through the eye of the hook and twist four times around the main line.

(2) From above, pull the spare end through the loop nearest the eye to form a bigger loop.

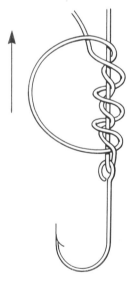

(3) Pass the end through the bigger loop, again from above, and coil it three times around the twisted strands. Lubricate and pull the end so that it is resting as far as possible from the hook.

(4) Lubricate again and pull on the main line to tighten the knot. Trim the spare end.

matchman's book and erect a large umbrella immediately behind where you are sitting. This will help to mask your movements from the fish and can be a very successful ploy.

As far as bait is concerned, I would suggest live sand-eels, pout or prawns. Bass will take other fish, but you will find that bright, lively ones are far better than species such as blennies or gobies. Sand smelts, herring or sprats are all good and have the added advantage of being able, when they are around, to be caught on the pole. The night before you go bass-fishing, simply tackle up with a tiny float and hook, baited with a small piece of fish, and drop it in the water beneath a harbour light. Keep a bucket and aerator handy and use it to keep alive the fish that you catch until you need them on the following day.

As well as bass, you will often find that garfish will take a free-lined livebait, as will pollack, although both seem to prefer to stay a little further out than the bass. Baits for garfish might be sand-eels or tiny pout, while pollack will take very small sand-eels or any size of prawn. If you drop a rubby-dubby (a mesh bag filled with pieces of fish, over which pilchard oil may have been poured) in the water, you will usually bring them within reach of the pole and, on many occasions, you will also tempt mackerel to come close enough to catch. This is particularly true on quiet days towards the top of the tide, when sand-eels would probably be the best bait to use.

For float-fishing it is best to keep things nice and simple, although you must be able to adjust the depth at which you are fishing to suit the state of the tide. A simple solution to this is to use sliding-float tackle complete with a stop tied out of red power gum as shown in the diagrams on page 44 and on this page. This will enable you to change your depth quickly and easily without damaging the line. To tie the stop simply lay a loop of power gum next to the line. Take one end and wrap it five times around both the loop and the line and then tuck it through the loop. Wet it and pull it tight from both ends. The diagram should make this clear. It is also a good idea to

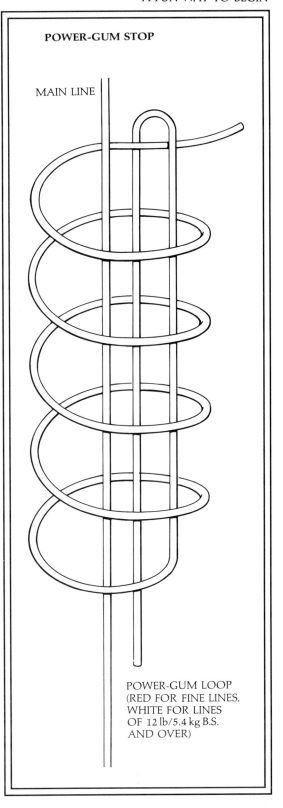

POWER-GUM STOP

MAIN LINE

POWER-GUM LOOP
(RED FOR FINE LINES,
WHITE FOR LINES
OF 12 lb/5.4 kg B.S.
AND OVER)

SLIDING-FLOAT RIG FOR POLES

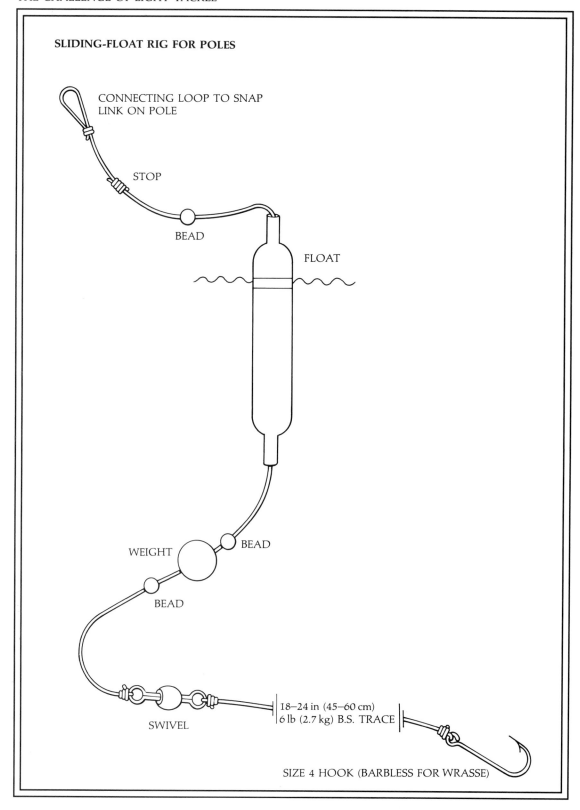

CONNECTING LOOP TO SNAP
LINK ON POLE

STOP

BEAD

FLOAT

WEIGHT

BEAD

BEAD

SWIVEL

18–24 in (45–60 cm)
6 lb (2.7 kg) B.S. TRACE

SIZE 4 HOOK (BARBLESS FOR WRASSE)

think about the type of hook that you are going to use. It is not necessary to use barbed hooks on the pole (with the exception of small Aberdeens for flatfish) and it is far kinder to use barbless ones. I personally like using Drennans in sizes 2 or 4 according to the bait that I am going to use. If you catch a wrasse it can be speedily returned to the water with the minimum of distress. Even deeply hooked fish can be returned if you take the hook out through the gills with a pair of forceps and then cut the hook from the trace. The fish is unharmed and all you need to do is to tie a new knot.

Float tackle has a variety of uses and is very effective for mackerel, garfish, wrasse and pollack. If you want wrasse then set your depth so that your weight is just off the bottom. Move 3 ft (90 cm) or so upwards for pollack or set your float 10–12 ft (3–3·7 m) deep for mackerel and garfish. Ragworm or prawns are both good for wrasse while prawns or mackerel strip will tempt pollack. If you want mackerel or garfish then use either live sand-eels or thin slivers of mackerel.

So far, all the tackles described have been intended for headlands or marks giving way to deeper water. Legering on the pole is quite different and, I would suggest, is primarily suitable for estuaries or flattie marks where the fish come close inshore. Certainly the marks where I have had the most success were at Salcombe or the River Teign. In both spots I caught most fish at the very bottom of the tide. I simply tackled up as for conventional leger – albeit with very light, non-toxic leads – and then dropped the bait as far out as I could. Bites were fairly decisive and I caught both flounders and plaice up to $1\frac{1}{2}$ lb (0·8 kg) in weight. The fight from the bigger ones was great fun, with the internal elastic being stretched to its limit on more than one occasion, while the best baits seemed to be ragworm tipped with the legs or claws from a peeler crab for plaice, or peeler on its own for the flounder.

Longer poles definitely have an advantage

If you use a pole, then even 2 lb (0.9 kg) wrasse put up a spectacular fight!

when legering, especially if they are fitted with internal elastic, and they can also be used at a greater range of marks than the shorter ones. You might, for example, use one to take a Starlite float-fishing in the winter for whiting from a pier, or to collect livebait or free-line for bass off a variety of marks. It therefore makes sense, if you are going to stick to one size of pole, to buy a 19 ft 8 in (6 m) telescopic and experiment. Alternatively, you might decide to try both the 19 ft 8 in (6 m) and the 13 ft (4 m) pole for livebait and wrasse. Whatever pole you eventually decide to use, you should find that pole-fishing, if nothing else, is usually some of the most enjoyable sport you can have. I hope you enjoy it as much as I do.

CHAPTER FOUR

FISHING ROCKY HEADLANDS

Standing precariously on one of the few rocks left uncovered by the tide, the angler gently and deliberately overcast the spot he wanted to fish. He paused, letting the line run through the float while it settled in the water, then softly drew it towards him, stopping every few seconds in case a fish might be following it in. Nothing happened, so he edged it closer to the hot spot, a narrow gully through which the tide ran with some force. Satisfied, he held the line back for a moment and then flicked the bale arm over so that it could run freely from the spool.

The tide had caught hold of the float now, whisking it into the gully while the angler's line, well coated with Mucilin to stop it from sinking, started to turn and follow it in. The angler watched, feeding the line between his fingers, then paused, expectant, as it neared the tail end of the little passage. Two things seemed to happen almost simultaneously: the float disappeared and the angler suddenly gripped the line tight and swept the rod into a satisfying arc. Almost at once a silver shape flashed below the surface, turned, and ran with considerable speed. The tip of the rod was pulled below the water and the drag of the reel started screaming.

Cautiously, because he was using a match rod and reel loaded with only 3 lb (1·4 kg) breaking-strain line, the angler extended the rod and tightened up the drag. The fish reacted angrily, tail-walking across the surface and then jumping clear to hit the water and dive. Once again it ran while the angler used side-strain to try and bring it under control. This seemed to have an effect. The fish broke the surface and then paused for a second, undulating as it seemed to consider what it ought to do next. Abruptly it surged forward and ran straight for the angler, almost taking him unawares, then changed its mind and ran parallel to the shore. Its flight was controlled so it changed direction, but it was tiring now; each time it ran or dived it took a little less line from the reel, until the angler checked the spool with his finger, then drew the fish towards him and brought it safely ashore.

Flapping angrily on the rocks, the garfish continued to struggle as it tried to reach the water. The next second it found itself wrapped in the soft folds of a dampened cloth as the hook was removed. For a moment it was admired, this much maligned and underrated species, and then it was slipped back into the water where it lunged forward and disappeared. The angler smiled and then reached upwards to change the depth of his float, setting it a little deeper than before, then re-baiting with a fresh sliver of mackerel.

Once again the angler drew the float towards his desired spot, but this time he missed the first bite, which shot the float below the surface and then abruptly let it go.

He tightened the line, waiting, and then struck on the second bite, reeling furiously as the mackerel turned and ran towards him, then changed direction, headed towards the surface, dived and ran again. The rod tip was drawn below the surface, but the angler was too experienced to be outwitted by the sudden turns of his prey. Instead he matched it move for move until the gleaming fish was brought safely ashore, dispatched and then put safely in a bag.

Over the next couple of hours the mackerel was joined by two or three of its brethren, while several others were returned to the water. Then a second fisherman appeared, brought out his beachcaster and lobbed out a 5 oz (142 g) weight clipped firmly to the end of his feathers. 'Got 'em!' he cried, grinning as he unceremoniously hauled three mackerel ashore and dumped them in a bucket. Once again he cast out and again three mackerel, with scarcely a flick of the tail, found themselves dragged ashore and dispatched. The fisherman turned round to speak to his companion, but he was already gone, disappearing up the hill as the sound of laughter heralded the arrival of the featherers, come to invest and claim this mark as their own.

* * *

Perhaps I may be accused of being cynical, but I always find it sad when people become obsessed with quantity, rather than quality of sport. Feathers are a prime example. In Torbay there are many headlands giving way to a very rich underwater environment. In the summer bass, flatfish, mullet, mackerel and garfish compete with John Dories, pollack, eels, congers and bream in a constant search for food.

In the early morning, when few people are around, you can enjoy some spectacular sport with light tackle, each fish fighting with such power and determination that the level of sport is very exciting. Bass make the occasional appearance on float while both mackerel and garfish seem to abound, interspersed with

Early-morning mackerel and wrasse from Hope's Nose in Torbay.

the occasional pollack. Meanwhile leger, cast accurately to particular hot spots, brings in flatties and a variety of other fish. Then the featherers arrive. Within minutes a constant succession of loud impacts on the surface of the water has driven all but the most

James Cleesby with a reasonable mullet.

determined of mackerel from the scene. The bottom seems barren and the rich variety that was there but moments before has fled before the constant barrage. The only people catching anything are a few people using float and the featherers, who do little more than simply winch in large numbers of mackerel on long-distance tackle.

The saddest part of this is the quality of the sport that is being overlooked. Too much activity tends to scare off the more cautious species, such as bass, and makes legering really hard work with comparatively little return. This is a pity as one of the main attractions of most headlands is that the rocks which surround them eventually give way to sand, creating a rich feeding ground for any number of species.

Predators can take advantage of any smaller creatures that emerge from cover, while on the sand itself there are worm-beds which no angler will ever be able to dig. Put the two together and you should create a rich and diverse menu which you will soon find will appeal to some very big fish.

If you choose your tackle and tactics carefully, you can enjoy some really good fishing, with the most productive times probably being early morning and evening, then on through the night. During the day the best thing to do is to place yourself well away from areas where there is a lot of activity and try to keep the noise to a minimum. This will considerably increase your chances of connecting with a better fish, many of which will be scared away from the busier spots by the numbers of lead weights impacting on the surface.

As to tactics, there are several methods that you might adopt, depending on both your position and the currents around the mark that you have chosen. The most popular ones will be spinning, legering or float-fishing in the summer or legering in the winter. Each of these methods will take several types of fish and can be easily improved by their conversion to light tackle.

The author plays a mackerel in light gear.

SPINNING

One of the delights of spinning is that it offers the light-tackle enthusiast a wonderful opportunity to experiment with different outfits. Carp rods and light fixed spools are very good, especially for distance work, but for sport *par excellence* the baitcaster really comes into its own. If you ever get the chance to try out a single-handed, pistol-grip baitcaster matched with a very light multiplier then I would earnestly suggest that you take it. The fight you get from each fish will more than justify the initial expense of such an outfit. Load the reel with 6 lb (2·7 kg) breaking-strain line, perhaps tipped with a 15 lb (6·8 kg) leader and you are ready to enjoy some breathtaking sport. As for lures, well, quite frankly, there are a number of lures on the market which all claim to catch any number of species. Some do, some don't; the important thing is to carry a selection of well-proven lures that will enable you to have the confidence to succeed, especially if you start to become frustrated during a period of extended inactivity. As with any method there are periods when you will not catch anything, simply because the fish will not be there. If they are around then spinning will catch as many as, if not more than, any other method. You simply have to be patient and make sure that your tactics match the time of day and state of tide. For example, if you are fishing a high tide in the early morning then there is a good chance that bass will be about. Why not experiment with plugs? These are heavy enough to cast on their own and often quite deadly, especially if the bass are already feeding on smaller species rather than crab. They are a lot of fun and catch some very big fish.

The only problem with plugs tends to be their expense; large Rapalas, for example, retail at over £10. They do cost a lot of money and you need to be sure that you are not going to lose very many. You also need to be sure that they will do their job and do it well, as you will not want to spend a lot of money on a lure that will never catch. The best thing is to buy one or two to start with and then add others as you identify the colours and shapes which work best in your area. Rapalas have a proven record of success, so they are probably the best to start with, but there are also quite a few others coming onto the market which are well worth having a look at, such as Damler and Eskimo plugs from DAM or even Jack Rapids from Ryobi.

Size and colour are both important, with colour probably the most variable from region to region. A plug that works well in Torbay, for example, might well be useless in Dorset. However, as a broad rule of thumb, I would tend to go for silver or metallic-coloured plugs in dull conditions, while on brighter days I would keep to either fluorescent orange or red. As for size, that will depend on the amount that you are prepared to invest. Larger

plugs are much more expensive than small ones, but they do catch more bass. If you want to catch a decent fish you will need a lure big enough to capture its interest. Bass are, after all, very efficient predators. They use much less energy in pursuing and catching one big meal than in chasing down several smaller ones. Apply the same logic to your plugs and you will not go far wrong.

On an early-morning session, the chances are that not too many other people will be around. This is quite an advantage as there will be less noise and you will not be restricted to casting straight ahead. You can explore the ground closer to shore, casting to both sides until you encounter fish. This is quite useful as bass tend to be closer in than many people might think. Should you hook one, make sure that your drag is set so that the fish can take line under pressure. A bass will usually run and, if it cannot take line, you have a good chance of being snapped. You will also need to be alert to sudden changes in direction. A good bass will often charge off in one direction and then abruptly swerve and swim straight towards you, shaking its head. This can lead to the hook being dislodged.

Once other people start to arrive, the chances are that the bass will move away. If the tide is quite high then it will probably pay you to change the plug for a spinner. If mackerel are about then bright, flashy silver lures are by far the best. There are many painted variations of each type of lure but, in all the years I have been fishing, I have never known a painted lure outperform a silver one for mackerel. Stick to silver lures and forget all the painted eyes and spots and everything else. These might make a difference for sea trout, for which you would need a licence, but they make no difference whatsoever for mackerel. The only exception is that it sometimes pays to have a gold or brass metallic spoon for days when the sun is fierce and the fish are feeding near the surface.

There are hundreds of spinners available but, if you stick to ABU Tobies, Daiwa

A catch of mackerel, pollack and garfish taken in Torbay.

Charlie used a baitcaster and closed-face reel to tempt these mackerel.

Crusaders, Cebars (which are brilliant for mackerel and also take the occasional bass), Weevers and Deltas, you will not go far wrong. All of these will catch fish, although the shape of the Cebar allows the angler to cast it just that little bit further out. Older anglers might recognize in it a marked similarity to the old German sprats you used to be able to buy.

Whichever lure you select, please bear in mind that they are designed to imitate the movements of smaller fish. Casting straight out and reeling in with no variations is not just very boring, but will also only catch a fraction of the fish that a varied retrieve will bring ashore. Make the lure come alive. Vary the speed at which you are working the spinner.

Get the rod tip low to the water and use it so the lure can dart forward, flutter back enticingly, then spurt away in a little burst of speed that will often trigger a bite. If you are using a Cebar, then dart it from side to side with tight, controlled movements of the rod. Reel in quickly, then slowly, flutter back, do whatever you think is sensible and whatever will make the lure more attractive to the fish. You will certainly catch more fish if you do.

Mackerel will bite best during the period both immediately before and after the high tide. They will also be caught at other states of the tide, but in nowhere the same quantity. If they really go off the feed, especially towards the low tide, then that might be a good time

Mackerel will often abandon caution in the evening and tear into spinners with near-suicidal ferocity.

Big mackerel will often take live sand-eels, particularly in the autumn.

to experiment for garfish. Take off the spinner and tie on a ball weight that has been adapted for spinning. You can thread the ball weight (otherwise known as a drilled bullet) directly onto the line if you wish, but you will find that the hard edges begin to severely abrade the line. If you buy a selection of ball weights and adapt them with stainless-steel links, you will find that your tackle losses drop dramatically. The same logic applies to float-fishing, although you will need to make sure that you adapt the right size of weight for the float that you will be using.

To adapt the weights you will need a vice, hacksaw, pliers and stainless-steel wire. Take a piece of wire, say about 4 in (100 mm) long, and turn the end of the wire back on itself to make a U-shaped bend. Trap this in a vice and coil the spare end about the wire to make an

eye. Cut off the surplus with a hacksaw, so that it is tightly trimmed to the remaining piece of wire, and then slide on a weight. Make a second eye — so that the weight lies between the two eyes — only this time slide a swivel onto the wire so that it is trapped on the finished eye. When you tackle-up, the main line will be tied to the first eye while a 3–4 ft (90–120 cm) trace will be tied to the swivel on the second. To the end of this trace will be attached a small hook baited with mackerel. The diagram on page 55 should make this clear.

The distance you cast will depend on the size of weight that you use. The heavier the weight, up to a certain point, the further you will cast. The only problem is that it is easier to work a lighter lead near the surface than a heavier one, and it is near the surface that the

ADAPTED BULLET FOR SPINNING

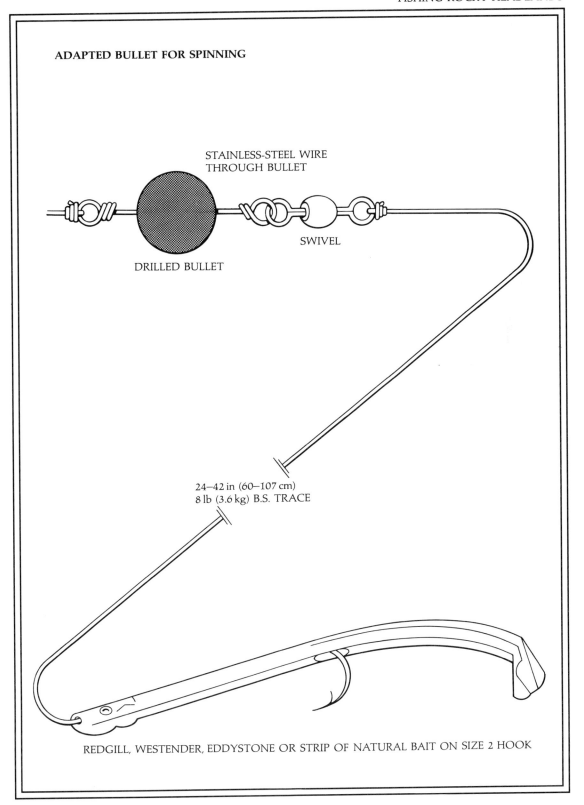

STAINLESS-STEEL WIRE
THROUGH BULLET

SWIVEL

DRILLED BULLET

24–42 in (60–107 cm)
8 lb (3.6 kg) B.S. TRACE

REDGILL, WESTENDER, EDDYSTONE OR STRIP OF NATURAL BAIT ON SIZE 2 HOOK

garfish will be found. Cast out and then retrieve the mackerel strip at a steady pace, allowing it to sink back every so often and then pulling it forward. If anything has been following it this will often induce a take. If you are trying this tactic in the evening, you will often find that it will also catch scad as well as garfish, although the latter will often stop biting a couple of hours before it gets really dark.

Once the evening starts drawing in you can either persevere with this tactic or change the mackerel strip for an artificial eel, such as a Westender, Redgill, Eddystone or Delta. This will tempt the occasional pollack or, in the winter, whiting. Work the eel fairly close to the bottom and go fairly slowly. As the evening gives way to night you can work the eel a bit faster so that it is lifted away from the bottom. As for the colour of the lure, it is often best to stick to grey in the evening, changing to a yellow eel when it is dark. You may also find that you catch the occasional school bass on this method, particularly if you are using Westenders.

FLOAT-FISHING
Step into the world of float-fishing and you will find yourself entering a domain of anticipation and almost breathless excitement. You find yourself watching, waiting, compelling the float to be drawn below the water as it drifts with the tide, the bait twirling, helpless, irresistibly in the view of the fish that you want to catch. For a while nothing happens, but then the float is swept below the water with such speed that you are taken unawares. A second bite follows, but this time you are ready, pulling into the fish and feeling it turn and run with your bait!

Done correctly, float-fishing is one of the most challenging and interesting methods available to the angler. It is a method that requires both skill and quick timing, testing your reflexes again and again, but it is also a method which is ideally suited to light tackle, promising a level of sport which only the

angler using it can enjoy to the full. You never know for sure what you are going to catch, which is part of its charm, but it presents your bait in a very favourable position for any number of species both by day and by night, for which you can buy special floats that have been made to take Starlites so you can continue your fishing for as long as you like.

Depth is, of course, also important. Go near the surface and you find yourself meeting the summer acrobat of our waters, the garfish. Its dives and sudden jumps provide spectacular sport on match rod and reels. It is also obliging, taking thin strips of mackerel with a joyous abandon that can leap your float out of the water and onto its side or sweep it beneath the surface so quickly you scarcely have the time to blink. Hit it straight away and you will find that you will have the pleasure not only of its fight, but also of watching it swim away. Delay and the garfish will usually manage to swallow the hook. It seems a pity to kill such a hard-fighting fish, so when it comes ashore simply open the gills with your finger, draw the hook through and cut it from the trace. This will then slip from its mouth and the hook can be re-tied at your leisure.

If you want a specimen garfish, a live sand-eel dangled anywhere from the surface to 15 ft (4·5 m) deep will often do the trick. It will also attract the attention of one of our other mini-predators, the colourful and obliging mackerel. It will usually signal its presence with a quick pull that speeds the float out of sight and a just as quick rejection of the bait. However, if you missed it the first time, then it will usually be happy to come back and give you a second chance to catch more than its attention.

Like the garfish, the mackerel is a pelagic species, generally swimming in the waters from mid-water to surface. It is a hard and fast fighter, but seldom attains any significant weight from the shore: a 2 lb (0·9 kg) fish is a specimen in almost any angler's book. Give it a chance on light tackle, using match rods close in or carp rods further out and it will oblige you with a spectacular display of

Garfish fight extremely well on light tackle. This one pulled Liam's rod into the water, after which we had a lot of fun trying to get it back!

sudden turns, dives and swift runs. Hit it on a baitcaster and you will wonder what on earth you have caught, especially if you fish near the bottom where the channel mackerel tend to run.

If you do go deeper, you will find other species begin to turn up. One of the most common will be pollack. This unassuming predator turns into a gladiator on a light enough outfit, running and diving with an abandon which it seldom if ever displays on heavier gear. It is also quite happy to take a variety of baits, including mackerel, garfish, squid strip or ragworm, although, as a broad rule of thumb, I would recommend sticking to either live sand-eels or prawns if you want the better fish.

It is also worth bearing in mind that rocky headlands are often the home of some very big bass. These give an excellent fight on light tackle, but they do demand a certain amount of dedication if you want to succeed on a regular basis. You need to give up a few hours' sleep and undertake a bit of research on the habits of the fish in your area. Bass, like many freshwater species, can become preoccupied with one source of food. If they are feeding on live pout, for example, you will have to catch a few for your bait, for which a pole is ideal. Then, if you do tempt a bass, it will often tip the float on its side and then draw it diagonally through the water. Turn the rod and pull into it hard enough to set the hook and it will reward your impudence with a fight that will tax even a carp rod. Hit it too early or too savagely and only the resurfacing of your float will mark where your bait met its end. The bass will be gone, slipping away through the water like a silver ghost in the twilight of dawn.

And, while we are on the subject of ghosts, let me introduce you to another favourite of light-tackle anglers, the grey mullet. This elusive fish appears and disappears like a phantom as it wills, but its reputation is misleading. Far from being almost impossible to catch, once the shoals become established in their regular summer haunts, they start to feed in regular and predictable patterns. They do, however, demand finesse if you want the best results. Your tackle must be scaled down to the lightest possible outfit, with match rods clearly the favourite for both performance and versatility. Scale your float down to perhaps an antenna or similar river float and tackle up with non-toxic split shot. Put on a tiny hook — say, anything smaller than an 8 — and you may find the local shoals giving your bread, mackerel flesh, maggot, steak, earthworm, harbour ragworm or other bait more than just a passing sniff. The diagram on page 59 should make the tackle clear, the only question mark perhaps being the use of silicon rubber. If you slide a piece of this on your line where you crimp the split shot, it will prevent the line from being damaged. This is important as, with lines lighter than 4 lb (1·8 kg) breaking strain, a big mullet will test its strength to the limits of its endurance. It will also keep its ace in reserve, namely that you must treat it with both respect and sensitivity, for behind its top lip is a membrane in which the hook often rests. If you are clumsy, this will split and the hook will come free, so to ensure your success you must treat it with light, deft hands, guiding it as gently and firmly as a horseman encourages a mount to the fence.

You can also take advantage of any natural groundbaiting going on in your area. If your headland has a sewer outfall, you will find that the mullet are, for reasons which I will not go into, already used to feeding on maggots, corn and bread. Later in the year, perhaps after the first of the autumn rains, you will find them feeding heavily upon worms which are swept down the drains. At these times you can make some very good catches by anticipating and matching the movements of your bait to the expectations of the fish. For example, there will be a regular, predictable current from the outfall. This may be influenced by the state of the tide, but you will find that the fish start to expect their meals to come from a particular direction. If you can trot your bait naturally

MULLET TACKLE

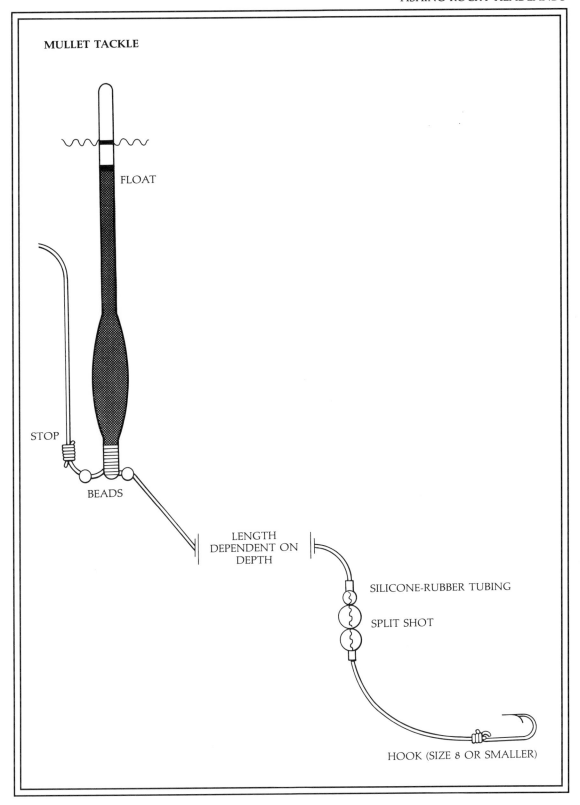

FLOAT

STOP

BEADS

LENGTH
DEPENDENT ON
DEPTH

SILICONE-RUBBER TUBING

SPLIT SHOT

HOOK (SIZE 8 OR SMALLER)

towards them – for which centre-pin reels and match rods are ideal – you will often find that a shoal has taken station behind a particular feature which it has learned to equate with food. If your bait is in the right spot at the right time, you should do quite well, provided that you were generous with your portion. Five maggots to a single hook is about right.

Moving back towards clearer and cleaner realms, as we approach the water immediately above the waving fronds of kelp, so we enter the domain of the wrasse. This delightful species, both colourful and obliging, will take a variety of baits and fight very well on appropriate tackle, making every effort to transfer your hook to the nearest piece of kelp. As it grows to over 10 lb (4·5 kg) with 6 lb (2·7 kg) fish a distinct possibility, you must approach both its home and its habits with

caution. Put away your match rod and go instead for a powerful carp rod, which will give you sufficient length and power to control and direct the powerful lunge of your prey.

Set the depth of the float to just off the bottom and watch carefully for bites. When you get a take you need to hit it fairly quickly, lifting the rod tip as high as you can and remembering that the first few seconds are the most important. Quick reflexes and decisive action will get the fish away from its immediate cover, where you will be able to fight and win the ensuing struggle in mid-water. Hesitate and the game will be lost. In the blink of an eye your tackle will be transferred to the weed and the wrasse will be gone, perhaps a little wiser, but not by very much. The next time it sees your ragworm, crab, prawn, razor-

When you unhook ballan wrasse, watch out for the dorsal spines.

fish or lugworm it will still be just as likely to charge on it straight away, sending your float below the water with a determined lunge on a bigger fish, or nervous jitters on a baby. Then, when you bring it ashore, why not weigh it, take a photograph and let it go? It is no use for eating but will be quite happy to reward your action by coming back to fight again, perhaps not this time, but certainly in the near future.

Finally, in this same region or just slightly above, there is one last summer migrant which I really ought to mention, particularly as it seems to be on the increase and the British record from shore is, as yet, unclaimed. That fish is the John Dory, a strangely beautiful fish which wends its way slowly towards its intended prey like a drifting piece of weed. Guile is the weapon of this species, which conceals its identity until the last moment,

when its telescopic mouth abruptly seals its victim's fate. It can be caught on rod and line, especially in August, but tends to be fairly small. Still, one day a 3 lb (1·4 kg) fish will claim both a tiny livebait and the British record and, I suspect, that will most probably happen on a deeply-rigged float fished very close to shore, certainly not more than 30 ft (9 m) away from the side of a headland. The bait will almost certainly be either a tiny live sand-eel or another equally small species, such as pout.

What else might you catch? That depends on where you fish. Coalfish will sometimes oblige, especially on sand-eels or whole sprats, and can be told apart from the pollack, which they closely resemble, by the fact that the lateral line is straight and its jaws are level. On the pollack the lateral line is curved over the

A nice coalfish taken in the late autumn.

pectoral fin and the bottom jaw protrudes beyond the upper. Eels — both conger and silver — will also appear on occasion, but you must return any silver eels if you do not have a licence for freshwater, this being the latest piece of nonsense from our bureaucratic brethren. As for the congers, which sometimes appear on deeply rigged livebaits, these are usually small males under 10 lb (4·5 kg) in weight. However, they do let you know in no uncertain terms that they are there. On mackerel strip, especially at night, you might find yourself taking scad — otherwise known as 'horse mackerel' — and, while these fight quite well on very light tackle, they are almost totally inedible and of very little use. In total contrast there are often occasions in summer when your float is subject to what appear to be phantom bites. It goes down, rather slowly and sometimes quite a long way, but then pops up upon striking as if nothing had happened. What you will probably be experiencing are bites from either squid or cuttlefish, both of which make extremely useful bait. The only way to hook them is to tie a 6 in (150 mm) long trace to the bend of your hook and then tie on a treble hook at the end. The squid grabs hold of the strip on your normal hook and a firm strike sets the trailing treble. Let it discharge its ink in the sea, pull it ashore and then kill it humanely in preparation for freezing down for bait. Chop it into several pieces if it is a big one and it will do several trips. Watch out for its bite, as it can be quite painful and similarly watch out for the venomous bite of the cuttlefish.

Another species you might encounter in summer is bream, which will sometimes turn up on both live prawn and tiny sand-eels fished very close to the bottom. Lastly, if you try float-fishing near the bottom in the winter, particularly at night, you may also encounter the occasional whiting.

So what tackle will you use? There are several rigs available with the most popular probably being the mullet rig illustrated on page 59, sliding-float tackle, and bubble or self-weighted carp floats for use with livebait. All are quite useful, with mullet tackle doubling for mackerel, garfish and catching small livebait on poles, while sliding-float tackle is perhaps the most versatile, especially with its facility for instantaneous changes of depth. If you use a drilled bullet that has been adapted as described in the section on spinning and set the tackle up as shown in the diagram on page 63, you will cut your tackle losses to a minimum. You will, however, also need to know how to tie a stop so that you can set the depth of the float. A suitable knot is described in Chapter 3, but it would be best if you tied it out of red power gum. This will slide on your line without damaging it and stay on for a considerable length of time, enabling you to make rapid changes of depth as often as you need to, for example when the tide begins to flood.

Self-weighted carp floats or bubble floats are useful for livebait, particularly if the part of the headland that you are fishing gives way onto a moderate depth of water. Which you use will depend on personal preference, depth and the distance that you need to cast. Bubble floats will predetermine the depth at which you can fish but will provide sufficient weight for long-distance casting. Self-weighted carp or pike floats do the same but can be rigged as for a sliding float so that you can fish at whatever depth you fancy. Their slimmer shape also provides much less resistance than a bubble float so that, when a fish takes your bait, you have a fraction longer before the bait is rejected, meaning that you hook more fish than might otherwise be the case. To carry out this adaptation simply thread on a bead, snap swivel and bead and tie on a swivel to your main line. The float is clipped to the snap swivel and the beads prevent this from passing over the stop. Lastly tie on a trace to the swivel on your main line, making this at least 3 ft (90 cm) long, preferably 4 ft (120 cm). The resulting tackle (see diagram on page 64) casts well and is particularly useful for bass.

Whichever rig you decide to use, there is

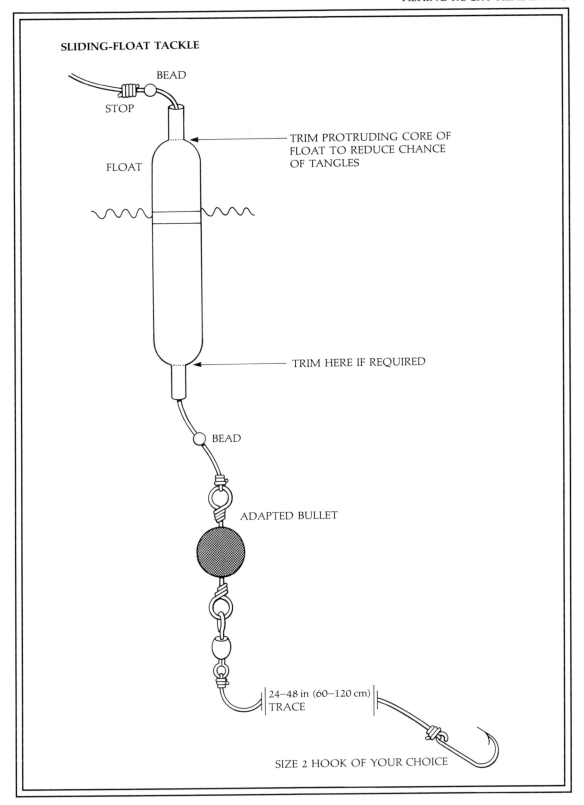

SLIDING-FLOAT TACKLE

BEAD

STOP

TRIM PROTRUDING CORE OF
FLOAT TO REDUCE CHANCE
OF TANGLES

FLOAT

TRIM HERE IF REQUIRED

BEAD

ADAPTED BULLET

24–48 in (60–120 cm)
TRACE

SIZE 2 HOOK OF YOUR CHOICE

LIVEBAIT TACKLE

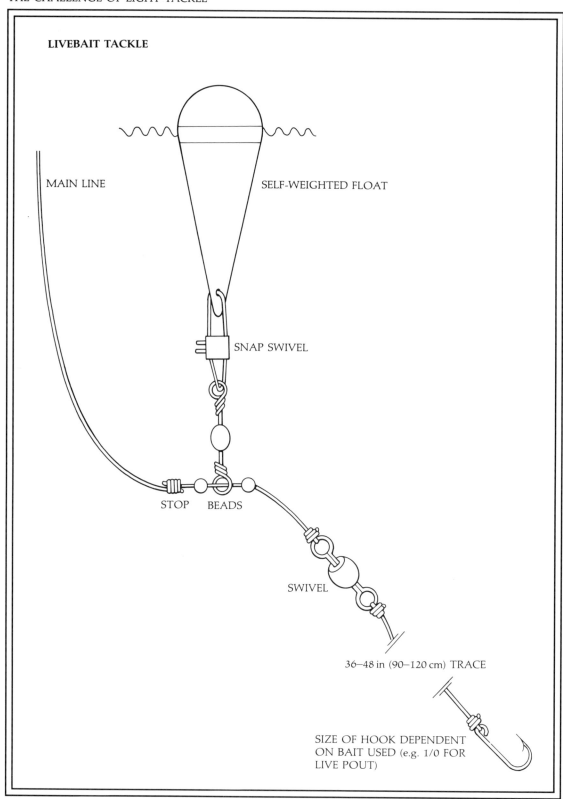

MAIN LINE

SELF-WEIGHTED FLOAT

SNAP SWIVEL

STOP   BEADS

SWIVEL

36–48 in (90–120 cm) TRACE

SIZE OF HOOK DEPENDENT
ON BAIT USED (e.g. 1/0 FOR
LIVE POUT)

one final point that should be made. When you use lighter tackle, you do not have the same hooking power that you have with heavier gear. If your hooks are sharp, that will not make the slightest bit of difference but, if they are blunt, then you could well find yourself missing bites. Get yourself a whetstone and sharpen your hooks. The cost of a whetstone is fairly minimal, but they do make a considerable difference to the number of fish that you catch. Ryobi, for example, make a whetstone that is attached to a retractable lanyard. This clips to your jumper and is always at hand without being in the way. It is a useful piece of equipment and well worth carrying, especially as it may make the difference between success or failure on a difficult day.

LEGERING

Looking out across the bay, the angler watched the tip of the rod being gently pulled in a series of little twitches, followed by a total lack of movement. Cautiously he eased the bail arm over, releasing a few feet of line and then knelt on one knee beside the tripod, hands ready to grip the rod and strike. For a moment nothing happened, but then two things seemed to happen so quickly that they almost blended together: the rod tip rattled vigorously and the angler struck.

Watching from the side, the rod tip seemed to be bent a little bit more than usual, albeit by not very much. Then, about halfway in, it started to take on a more satisfying curve and was abruptly pulled back as whatever was on the end made a determined lunge for the bottom, taking a little bit of line against the drag. The angler responded by lifting the rod as high as possible, forcing the fish grudgingly away from the bottom. It responded, but the line went slack and then tight as the fish experimented to see where it could run.

By now there were two or three anglers watching, waiting for the golden-brown flash we expected as the flatfish was drawn into view. Then, suddenly, there it was! A lovely dab in excess of 1 lb (0·5 kg) turning abruptly on its tail and diving back towards the bottom as it, too, caught its first sight of us. This happened several times, the fish running away with whatever line the angler gained until it was finally guided over the rim of the waiting net and swept ashore. Then we all gathered round to admire it, a superb autumn fish in prime condition and weighing just over $1\frac{1}{2}$ lb (0·8 kg).

The lucky angler grinned and then ran his hands over the fish to check its identity. No, the skin was not smooth all over, so it was not a plaice; there were no tubercles along the base of its fins or on the head so it was not a flounder; but, as the skin felt rough when he rubbed it from tail to head, it was, quite definitely, a specimen dab. Satisfied, he grinned at us, deftly unhooked it and placed it in a pool where it joined another two of its brethren. Then he re-baited with half a peeler crab and re-cast to the same spot, the point where the rocks gave way to sand about 80 yd (75 m) out.

This time, after a few minutes waiting, the bite when it came was quite different: a hard and fast rattle which he immediately struck. The fish also felt heavy all the way in, not fighting very hard but occasionally putting a good bend in the rod as it ran against the pressure from the shore. Then, when it appeared, more than one of us smiled, watching the glorious colours of the spread pectoral fins as the gurnard glided up in the wake of the lead. It grunted as we unhooked it, but with powerful flicks of its tail sped back to the depths the instant it was placed back in the sea.

As this particular angler found, one of the beauties of legering with light tackle is that even small fish feel much larger than they do on conventional gear. Another is the variety of fish that can be taken close to headlands, including bass, gurnard, dogfish, plaice, flounders, dabs, whiting, red mullet, eels, bream, cod in the winter and rays. All of these fight well on carp, pike or bass rods although, if you expect double-figure rays or cod, it would be wise to step up to a 3 lb (1·4 kg) test-curve pike rod matched with a multiplier such as a Daiwa Millionaire. This will handle quite heavy fish and still give an excellent fight. It will also handle heavyweight wrasse if you cast into the weeds rather than further out on the sand.

Casting on this tackle needs as much skill as casting with a beachcaster, especially if you want to reach a distance in excess of 100 yd (90 m) with the much lighter leads you can use. If you can cast 125 yd (115 m) with a 3 oz (85 g) lead weight, then you can cast as far as you need to for the majority of headlands you are ever likely to encounter. The chances are that, if you can cast 80 yd (7 m) with a 2 oz (57 g) spiked lead, that will be all the distance you need. Certainly one of the dangers of legering is that people become preoccupied with distance. What is the point of casting beyond where the fish are likely to lie? The most productive spots will either be where the rocks give way to sand, usually between 30 and 90 yd (27 and 80 m) out, or where there is a sand or gravel patch in the middle of the rocks. Such spots can be deadly for flatfish and rays, primarily because that is where they can find both a greater variety and quantity of food. Cast beyond that and you will still catch the occasional fish, but you will be missing out on the attraction that brings fish to the headland in the first place. You might just as well go and fish off the beach!

Use the headland, both its shape and its currents, to catch the maximum variety of fish. At its point the currents will often be fierce. Predators will be hunting for fish being swept along in their grip. Look out for gullies. Smaller fish will be channelled into these by the currents and make easy prey for predators waiting at the opposite end. Alternatively, where the bottom becomes mostly sandy, the hunters will cover as much ground as they can, searching constantly for food. At that point you must decide whether to let your tackle do the same, for example, to use an Aquazoom

lead so that it travels with the current, or fix the bait in position with a spiked lead in the hope of setting up a scent trail that will draw fish to the hook.

Work out your strategy with a tide-table close to hand. Many of the smaller species will go to ground at high tide, hiding until the tide has turned and is well on its way down. This is the time for the predatory fish. Forget your small hooks and baits. Put on a livebait and a rolling weight for bass, or a whole squid or several lugworm for cod if you are fishing in the winter, and stay close to your rod, waiting to strike instantly the moment a decisive bite appears. Then, at low tide, flatfish, dogfish and gurnard will come on the feed and binge for an hour or so. Lighter weights and small Aberdeens tipped with peeler crabs or ragworm will tempt the flatfish, while peeler or small strips of fish will tempt gurnard.

If you want dogfish — and this much-maligned species fights well on lighter rods — then forget subtlety and put on a 2/0 hook baited with either a whole or a half *calamari* squid, or a long, broad strip of mackerel. You may also find on occasion that bull huss — otherwise known as 'greater spotted dogfish' — are feeding in the areas that you are fishing, in which case fresh mackerel will have a distinct advantage over squid. They are usually a lot bigger than lesser spotteds, but if you do get two roughly the same size then you can tell them apart by looking at the nasal flaps. The bull huss has a single, large nasal flap as opposed to two that are small and so tightly tucked that they appear to be slits rather than flaps. They fight a lot harder than lesser spotteds and will put a considerable curve in the rod. You will almost certainly have to pump part of the way, reeling in while simultaneously lowering the rod tip to the water and then locking the spool with your thumb and forcing the rod up. This usually happens in the later stages of the fight, although you would be wise to be prepared to give line at any time should the fish decide to run. This should then enable you to keep in control.

Dogfish often abound around headlands, feeding actively at night.

If you are fishing at night, a leger baited with mackerel strip will also take pouting in summer and whiting in winter, with three-bearded rockling sometimes making an appearance at any time of the year. There will be a lot of smaller fish among them which will delight in taking any smaller offerings that you might care to make. So, if you want to catch a decent fish, think big. Small strips that imitate fry are all well and good for mackerel on float-fishing tackle, but on the bottom, if you want bigger fish, you must catch their attention with a much larger bait. If you do not you will be pestered by tiny fish and have little to show for your efforts at the end of the night. Even with large baits, you will still catch a fair share of smaller fish, but at least they will weigh around the pound mark instead of just a few ounces!

When you are using bigger baits, the most efficient end tackle is the leger itself, as opposed to a multi-hook paternoster which has little relevance to rocky headlands. If you look at the diagram on page 69, you will see this depicted; the only obvious difference from conventional arrangements is the short piece of tubing I use to separate the lead from the swivel. This helps prevent tangles, particularly if you decide to use a spiked lead rather than a plain one and is very inexpensive, a packet sufficient for 25 lengths costing well under £1. They are usually sold in packets of five long tubes, which you can cut to the size required by rotating the tube on a very sharp knife and then rubbing the ends lightly on fine emery paper to prevent the line being abraded. If you cut some of the tubes into 3 in (75 mm) sections and others into pieces 1 in (25 mm) long, you will find the longer ones useful for legers and the shorter ones ideal for paternosters.

If you decide to do a lot of fishing at night, it will pay you to invest in a tripod, headlamp, Tilley lamp and thermal suit. These will enable you to fish in moderate comfort, making each outing fun rather than a test of endurance. If you put your tackle into a seat box it will also give you something comfortable to sit on, which is much better than developing piles from being constantly perched on the rocks. Another item you should buy is a gaff. From time to time you will catch fish that a net just will not be able to manage. A gaff is the only tool to use, particularly if you decide to try for conger, which often abound around the ends of such headlands. If you do, though, you will need to step up your tackle. If the conger are small, a 12 lb (5·4 kg) boat rod, such as the Ryobi Project P12 matched to a multiplier, such as the SL220, will handle them if you are fast and determined in the way that you fight.

Now people might laugh at using such a light rod for conger, but it will handle the majority of the eels that you are likely to catch from the shore, especially if the headland gives way immediately to sand so that you can fight the eel over a comparatively clear bottom. When I tested this type of outfit, I secured a spring balance to the floor and pulled into it as hard as I could. The rod enabled me to put a full 12 lb (5·4 kg) of pressure on the balance and I was able to maintain this for some time without undue discomfort. Next I attached an uptide boatcaster to the balance, where considerable effort was needed to make it register to 10 lb (4·5 kg) for even short periods of time. After that I tried a 30 lb (13·6 kg) outfit followed by an 80 lb (36·3 kg). The 30 lb (13·6 kg), with a lot of effort, pulled the scales to 18 lb (8·2 kg) while the heavy outfit only registered a few extra pounds at 23 lb (10·4 kg). In neither case was I able to maintain the steady pressure that I had been able to exert on the lighter outfit. Despite the fact that they were much heavier than the 12 lb (5·4 kg) class outfit — and consequently more uncomfortable to use — the extra pull available was not worth the extra effort involved.

As far as end tackle is concerned, conger gear is essentially a stepped-up leger, as illustrated on page 70. However, because the conger has such a powerful bite, you will need to make the trace out of at least 30 lb (13·6 kg) breaking-strain nylon-covered wire or 120 lb (54·4 kg) commercial nylon, tying it with

LEGER

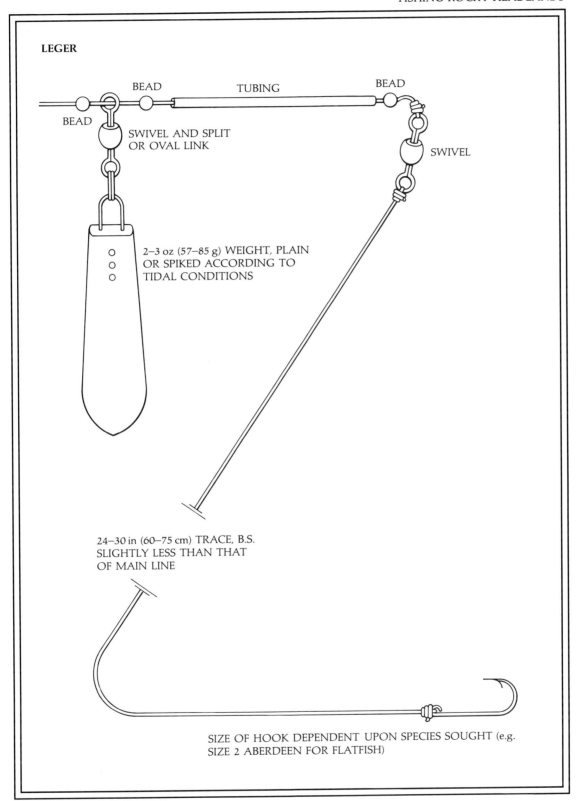

BEAD

BEAD

TUBING

BEAD

BEAD

SWIVEL AND SPLIT
OR OVAL LINK

SWIVEL

2–3 oz (57–85 g) WEIGHT, PLAIN
OR SPIKED ACCORDING TO
TIDAL CONDITIONS

24–30 in (60–75 cm) TRACE, B.S.
SLIGHTLY LESS THAN THAT
OF MAIN LINE

SIZE OF HOOK DEPENDENT UPON SPECIES SOUGHT (e.g.
SIZE 2 ABERDEEN FOR FLATFISH)

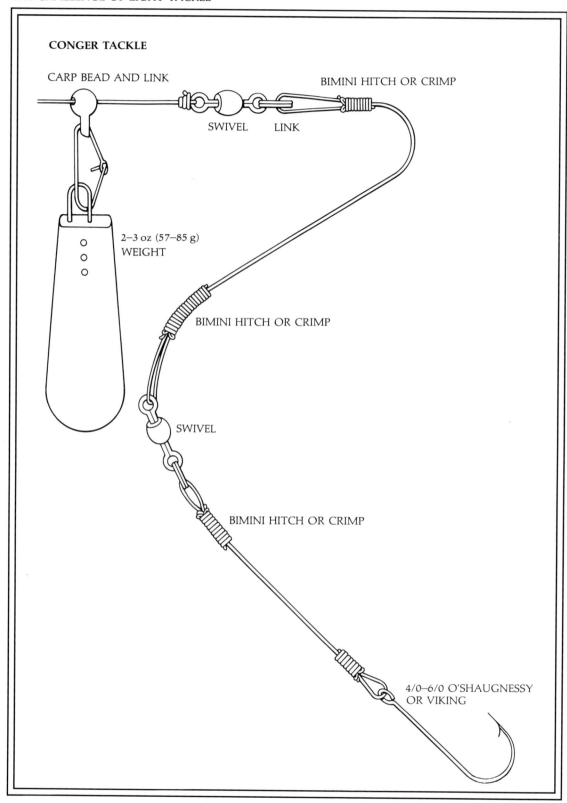

CONGER TACKLE

CARP BEAD AND LINK

BIMINI HITCH OR CRIMP

SWIVEL   LINK

2–3 oz (57–85 g)
WEIGHT

BIMINI HITCH OR CRIMP

SWIVEL

BIMINI HITCH OR CRIMP

4/0–6/0 O'SHAUGNESSY
OR VIKING

either crimps or the bimini hitch. Use at least two fairly large swivels and make sure the trace is no longer than 18–24 in (30–60 cm) maximum, as long traces increase the chance of the conger reaching cover. You would also be advised to use 18–20 lb (8·2–9·1 kg) main line on the reel, so that the loss in strength from tying your knots does not interfere with the pressure you can exert from the rod. A poorly tied knot will, for example, break at half the breaking strain of the line. A 20 lb (9·1 kg) line, under pressure but well tied, will break at around 15 lb (6·8 kg), which is above the pressure that a light outfit can maintain. Bait up with a fillet of mackerel and you are ready to begin, casting your tackle only a very short distance from the shore. Alternatively use a flapper, which is a mackerel with the backbone removed and the fillets left dangling from the head. This is very popular in the south of England and is also useful for skate.

When a conger bites, it will usually back away from the rod, taking line from the reel and then stopping. Strike at this point and you will usually lose the fish. It will try to turn the bait, in order to swallow it, and then move away a second time. This is the time to strike and then to pump furiously to get it up and away from the bottom. Get it up and it will often spin and fight on the surface, making occasional dives which you should be able to control. Leave it too long and it will get in among the rocks where you would need a crane, not a rod, to get it out! However, if you are successful, bring it to the side, gaff it and get it out of the water as quickly as possible. It is important now to act surely but with care.

Kill it humanely with two powerful blows to the head and tail vent and then leave the hook alone until you know for certain that the eel is dead and not merely stunned! After all it is much easier to tie on a new hook than replace bitten fingers! If you use links in your tackle, as shown in the diagram, you can prepare extra traces in advance and simply clip them on as you need them. There will be little inconvenience and you will at least be safe, which brings me to the last point I wish to make, namely taking care to be sure that you are safe when you fish in these isolated spots.

You see, all things considered, rocky headlands probably give the angler his or her best chance of connecting with a specimen fish from the shore. They are rich in marine life and they are also often areas of outstanding natural beauty, where it can be a joy to fish. Please visit them, but be sure to let someone know where you are going, particularly if the weather looks a little dicey. At night, when there are other people around and the air is filled with the soft murmur of voices and the sparkle of Tilley lamps, they can be deceptively peaceful and compelling. However, an unexpected wave at the wrong moment can change this idyllic scene to a tragedy, so please take care because headlands, although they are lovely, can also be wild and untamed. Enjoy your trip, but err on the side of caution and take another person along. If nothing else they can always gaff any congers and, in an emergency, they may well be your only hope, just as you might well be theirs. As the scouts say, 'be prepared' and consequently stay safe to enjoy your trip to the full.

CHAPTER FIVE

FISHING FROM THE BEACH

Imagine it is summer, then cast a fleeting glance over a beach at low tide. Sunlight glistens on the gleaming bodies of indolent sleepers while the screeches of children mingle with the cries of the seagulls as they glide overhead or descend to strut along the sand. Laughter fills the air, while the background murmur of the sea is lost in the babble of voices, both human and bird. Swimmers sport in the waves while small children dig vigorously in search of hidden treasures in the sand. There is much going on.

Then, as night falls and the tide begins to rise, so creatures hidden from our view emerge to feed and, in turn, be fed upon by flatfish and other predators. Lugworm, silver ragworm, razorfish and clams slide cautiously from their burrows while in other places the sand suddenly erupts as clouds of sandeels fling themselves forward from their places of concealment. A variety of crabs dig themselves laboriously from where they lay hidden and are swiftly joined by sand shrimps and tiny flatfish.

For a while, as the tide slowly rises, these creatures are left in relative tranquillity. Shore crabs kill and eat a few flatfish, amongst other things, but by and large there is little to make them seriously alarmed. This is, however, merely the lull before the storm. The depth continues to increase and, as if on cue, the silvery shapes of bass suddenly dominate the scene, seizing unwary prey as they hunt in water as little as 30 yd (27 m) from the shore. Larger flatfish appear, scooping up whatever

worms they can find, while further out the weird silhouette of a ray glides menacingly towards an injured sand-eel left behind by the other members of its shoal.

At the end of the beach, where the sand is broken by the rocks, sole begin to emerge and hunt around the edges of the sand. Swiftly, under cover of the encroaching darkness, they are swarmed over and hidden by the sudden appearance of a large shoal of pout. For a while they compete against each other in their search for food, but abruptly the shoal of pout wheels, alarmed by a sudden impact on the surface of the water. For a moment they flee, but there is no recurrence and gradually their curiosity overcomes their sense of fear, especially as there is now a strong scent of injured worms to spur them on. They gulp the water quickly, passing it over olfactory organs tuned to identify direction, and then several turn at once, each racing to be the first to reach what they perceive to be an easy meal.

Standing on the shore, the solitary angler noticed first one series of tugs, then another. He grunted and struck swiftly, neatly hooking the unlucky pout that was taking his bait, reeling it quickly ashore and dropping it in a large bucket of water which was being aerated. A minute or two later it was joined by another and then another, until there was a small shoal of pout in the bucket, each some 4–5 in (100–125 mm) long and just about the perfect size for livebait.

Having gathered enough pout for his bait, the angler checked his watch. It was now nearing midnight, with just over an hour before the high tide. Perfect. With a nod of satisfaction he changed the rod he was using for a pike rod. This was tackled-up with running leger to a fairly large hook, which he passed through the upper jaw of one of the pout. Next he aimed carefully at a spot where the rocks were broken by a large patch of sand and then cast as gently as possible towards the spot that he had chosen.

For a while little happened. The angler tightened his line and then waited, tethering the pout in the open. Occasionally he moved the lead a foot or so towards him, kicking up a little puff of sand, but apart from that he did nothing, simply holding the rod as he waited for a bite that may have come in minutes or may not have come at all.

The bite, when it finally came, was not at all what he expected. Instead of a decisive lunge there was a series of twitches, almost taps, spaced some seconds apart, as if something was shuffling itself over the bait. Then there was nothing, no movement whatsoever. He waited to see what was happening and then swept the rod sideways and up as the line tightened and began to move away, tightening the drag on the multiplier he was using so that he could increase the amount of pressure he was able to exert. This set the hook firmly, and the fish responded by surging away with what appeared to be violent lunges. When this was controlled it settled to ground, swimming close to the floor as it was forced, slowly, to head towards the shore.

The angler, feeling the weight of the fish, pumped the rod as he brought the fish closer, locking both hands on the rod, lifting upwards and then reeling in quickly as he lowered the tip. The fish suddenly surged away in protest, taking line against the drag, but was gradually forced back again until the angler could bring it ashore and identify it: a small-eyed ray on a beach where he had never heard of a ray being caught.

*   *   *

On this particular occasion the angler that I watched was surprised as he only expected bass. He had been unaware that there were other predators on the beach he was fishing. However, by offering a bait which was natural to the beach, as opposed to importing a different bait from another area, he actually made his tackle far more attractive than might otherwise have been the case. The fish he tempted was already accustomed to feeding on the shoals of pout which were a regular, almost permanent, feature of this particular spot. It had become *preoccupied* with them, a term anglers use to describe a fish that seems to lose interest in feeding upon anything other than a very specific bait. Pout had become its almost exclusive diet.

If the angler had offered sand-eels at this particular spot, he may or may not have been lucky with the bass, but I doubt whether he would have caught this particular ray. When he gutted it the only recognizable contents of its stomach were pout, which reinforces the point that I wish to make: if you are fishing from a beach, it will pay you to use bait similar to that upon which the fish are already feeding. The best way of doing that is to plan two trips to the beach.

The first trip, which is essentially a mapping expedition, will be at low tide, when you can identify patches of natural food and features which may affect your fishing. This may comprise lugworm and razorfish beds, patches of silver ragworm and, for example, a freshwater stream. If there is such a stream, you may well find that it is a natural draw for shoals of sandeels, in which case it will also attract bass. Other features, such as breakwaters, may deflect currents and set up holding areas for food. Imagine, if you like, that you are a saltwater-detective on the lookout for clues. Once you find them, they will help to make any map that you draw far more useful than a mere list of what is where and how far it is from the high-tide line. Remember that the beach is a balanced and viable environment. If you focus on one particular aspect, you may lose sight of what else it has to offer. At this stage it is far better to make the map as comprehensive as possible. You can always focus on individual species later. It will also pay you to collect some samples of the creatures that you find, which you will need for the second trip.

The best time for this second trip, at least in my opinion, will be at night, at high tide, with the worms or whatever that you collected earlier. Place them upon very small hooks, size 6 Aberdeens or smaller, and then cast to the spots that you identified earlier. See what takes your bait. If there is a profusion of smaller fish, these may well be the main diet of the local predators. Keep a bucket handy and pop in what you catch. You may find lots of pout feeding on sand shrimps. Put on one of those pout for bait and you could well find yourself connecting with a bass or some other predator. You may also find yourself having a few surprises, as happened on the night when I went to a particular beach which was noted for its bass. A skindiver entered the water and, swimming no more than 20 yd (18 m) from the shore, pulled out five sole which were well over 2 lb (0·9 kg) in weight, capped by a really big one that went just over 4 lb (1·8 kg). No one had ever mentioned that there were such big sole on this particular beach, which is probably a fair indication that it was not widely known. As for those few who did know, how many would have felt comfortable casting only 20 yd (18 m) from the shore? Be honest about it. There is considerable peer pressure to fish at long range, regardless of whether or not this is actually the best range at which to fish. Anyone coming down and blasting out their baits would have completely missed the very fish they were after. However, if they planned their initial trips properly, experimenting with baits placed from 10 yd (9 m) to over 100 yd (90 m) from the shore, then they would have a very good indication of just where the fish were feeding and exactly what types of fish were available.

Following your initial trips, you will find

that each and every subsequent trip will add to your knowledge of your chosen beach. You will have made a good beginning, but you will still find some other surprises turning up from time to time, especially if you vary your tackle and bait. For example, on one of my local beaches I used both leger and float tackle, including self-weighted Drennan Crystal Missiles set up for mullet, to catch a variety of species, including silver eels, bass, plaice, sole, dabs, flounders, mackerel, garfish, black bream, whiting, pout, grey gurnard and mullet.

Another fish which occasionally turned up was the lesser weever, a venomous fish which is prolific on some beaches and which ventures very close to the shore. Now weevers are definitely something you should be wary of. There are two species — greater and lesser — living in British waters, and both have an extremely painful sting. The poison is delivered through the sharp dorsal spines and can lead to several hours of intense discomfort. If they are common on your beach, I would seriously recommend that you get yourself a pair of forceps and a pair of sturdy workman's gloves to hold the fish while you unhook it. The expense will be negligible compared to the discomfort you will experience if you do end up being stung!

As for the other fish that I mentioned, well, if you want to catch a variety of species, you can improve your chances in several ways. Here are ten tips which you might find useful.

1   When there is a bit of surf running in the summer, set up a running leger with a reasonable size hook (say a 2/0 Aberdeen or Viking) and cast out either a live sandeel or several razorfish for bass. Aim to hit the water just behind the third breaker.

2   If you are using a fixed-spool reel and you have found where the fish are, take a loop of line from your reel and trap it behind the line clip on the spool. This will ensure that you reach the same spot every time, stopping the line if you accidentally overcast.

A specimen garfish from Brixham.

3 Razorfish are a good bait for a number of species and are prolific on some beaches. You can collect them at low tide by finding the keyhole-shaped openings to their burrows and then either digging them up or squirting a strong solution of saltwater into the burrow. This brings them to the surface where you can pick them up. You should, however, be aware that where there is one razorfish there are often many others. Most of these will have no visible signs of their presence. If you dig out in a circle from where you found the first one, you will often collect many more. On the last occasion I found 50 razorfish where I had seen only one burrow in the sand. I also found hundreds of tiny clams, perhaps a dozen sandeels and about 30 silver ragworm.

4 If you want to use paternoster tackle for distance work, stick to small hooks in the summer — say size 4 or even 6 Aberdeens — and bait them with silver ragworm or lug. A wishbone-cum-pulley rig, as illustrated on page 78, will give you fewer tangles than some other rigs, but you will need some telephone-wire stops. Make these by taking the fine inner wires of telephone cable and wrapping them around a nail or coathanger to the desired length. Slide them onto the main line and twist between thumb and forefinger until they stay in place.

5 Leger tackle is a very efficient method for catching big predators, but it is wasted if you use it with tiny baits, unless you are going for flatfish or sole, which hug the bottom. It is best used in conjunction with a fairly large bait, say live sandeels or pout, while in the winter it can be matched with a pennel rig to collect livebait on the spot, so to speak. Pennel rigs are easy to make and are essentially just a tiny, worm-baited hook tied on a very short trace to the bend of a much bigger hook. It is often a good tactic for sorting out the larger cod in the winter and bass in the summer,

acting just like a hair rig and presenting the hook in an excellent position for striking.

6 If you are after bass and you find a load of drifting seaweed when you get to the beach, just get back in your car and go somewhere else. You will catch far more bass — and enjoy the fishing more — if you go to where the beach is clear. After all, there is precious little enjoyment to be gleaned from endlessly picking seaweed off your line!

7 If you decide to go for cod in the winter, rig up a streamlined paternoster and make your bait as large as possible, say five, or even six, black lugworm on the trace. Cod seem to appreciate a big bait, but on lighter tackle you will need to restrict yourself to just the one hook. Light bass or pike rods are fine for any number of beaches but, if the beach you want to fish slopes only gradually into deeper water, you would do better to find a light beach-caster instead. As a broad rule of thumb you should find that bass rods will give you a maximum range of 100–125 yd (90–115 m) while above that you really need a beachcaster.

8 When you use paternoster tackle, put a small bead and stop on the trace above the bait. This stops air resistance sliding the bait up and away from the hook during the cast.

9 Always fish near a feature if you can. This might be anything from a pier to a break-water, or even a freshwater stream, but in the long run you will find that it pays. If you cannot spot any obvious features, then fish at either end of the beach, where the water meets either rocks or the cliffs. The chances are that there will be rocks around the base which will provide shelter for any number of smaller creatures, such as peeler crabs or prawns, drawing preda-tors from miles around. If you cast at the edges of these rocks, you may well find a greater variety of species coming to your hook than you might otherwise expect.

BLOOD-BIGHT LOOP

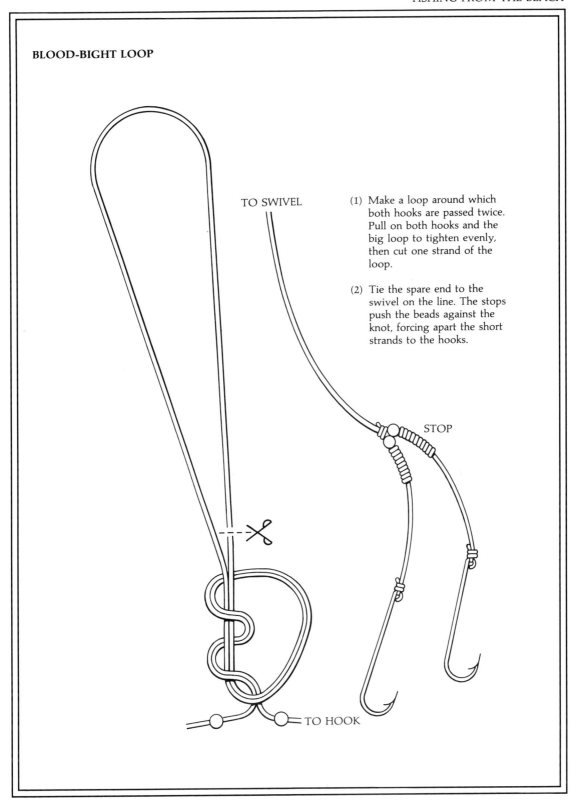

TO SWIVEL

TO HOOK

STOP

(1) Make a loop around which both hooks are passed twice. Pull on both hooks and the big loop to tighten evenly, then cut one strand of the loop.

(2) Tie the spare end to the swivel on the line. The stops push the beads against the knot, forcing apart the short strands to the hooks.

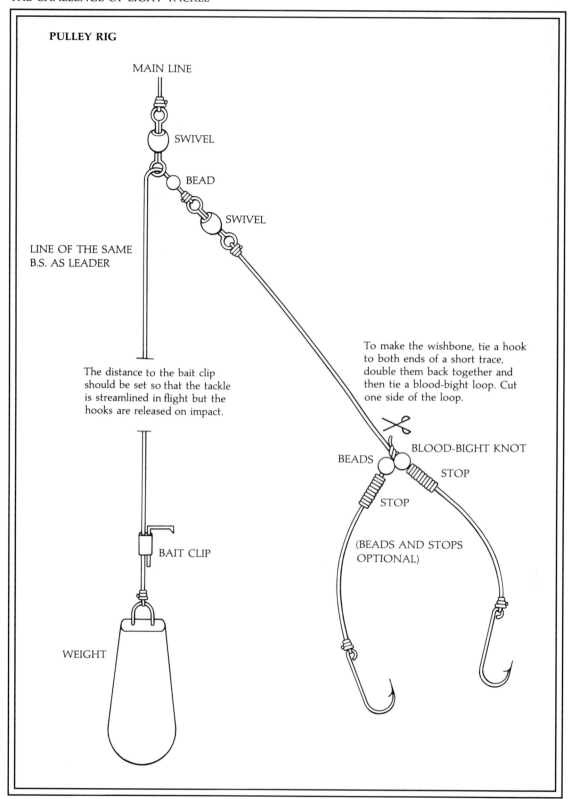

PULLEY RIG

MAIN LINE

SWIVEL

BEAD

SWIVEL

LINE OF THE SAME
B.S. AS LEADER

The distance to the bait clip
should be set so that the tackle
is streamlined in flight but the
hooks are released on impact.

To make the wishbone, tie a hook
to both ends of a short trace,
double them back together and
then tie a blood-bight loop. Cut
one side of the loop.

BLOOD-BIGHT KNOT

BEADS

STOP

STOP

(BEADS AND STOPS
OPTIONAL)

BAIT CLIP

WEIGHT

If you fish close to the rocks, you will often find that pollack will appear on both leger and float.

10 Give float tackle or spinning the occasional try. During the summer there are often large shoals of mackerel off beaches, especially in the early morning when they seem to feed very actively. If your beach gives way into deeper water then either method will also catch the occasional pollack or bass.

I hope these tips prove useful, but another point I ought to mention is that all of the methods which I have so far described work very well off exposed or open beaches. If you live near a beach with a sea wall running along part of its length, you will find that not only do all of these methods work, but also that the increased depth of water will enable you to experiment with much lighter tackle than you might otherwise expect, especially if there are sections of the wall where the sand or shingle is seldom or never exposed at the low tide. From marks such as this you can scale your tackle right down and see what comes up.

Swanage in Dorset is a good example. There is a slipway to one side of the beach where there is a good depth of water at high tide. From here it is possible to fish with a $\frac{1}{2}$ oz (14 g) non-toxic weight set up on a freshwater legering rod. During the day there is little to interest the angler, but at night there are quite a few flatfish, which give an excellent fight on the lighter tackle, and you will also come across the occasional eel. The only frustration you will find is that this spot seems to be invested with an enormous population of crabs, which seems to be a talking point in the town and which draws children from miles around with their handlines! Certainly it distracted my children, who ended up 'crabbing' in one corner while I went fishing in another. By any accounts though it certainly is a nice place to fish and while you are there you may even find yourself, as I did, watching the eager youngsters with a pang of nostalgia for the memory of the days when, as a child, I would persuade my mother or father to let me do just the same thing.

On marks such as this you will also find that, in the summer, there is often a healthy population of mullet. On one beach in Torbay I have often watched huge shoals of mullet gathering in March or April, depending on the temperature, prior to splitting up and dispersing round the bay. I have rarely caught any of these fish at this time, although later in the season they do seem to be easier to catch. One thing I did find, however, was that it sometimes paid to be able to offer two baits instead of one. It was also useful to be able to overcast the shoal and then reel back gently without disturbing the fish. This was quite a useful tactic which was made possible when I discovered Drennan's self-weighted Crystal Missiles in one of my local tackle shops. The thing I like about them is that they are large enough to see without discomfort and that their loading still enables you to put a tiny, non-toxic lead on the line without sinking the float, so you do not have to fiddle about with split shot. They can be adapted to sliding-float tackle and are sufficiently heavy to be cast a significant distance on a match rod, say 50 yd (45 m) or perhaps a little more.

To set up the tackle you will need a treble swivel, the lightest of the non-toxic ball weights, a couple of tiny beads, a swivel, the float and some 6 lb (2.7 kg) breaking-strain line. You start by sliding on a bead, the float and a second bead and then tie on a normal swivel. This is necessary to stop the float getting entangled in the traces. Tie a 3 ft (90 cm) section of nylon to the other eye, slide on the weight and then tie the nylon to the middle eye of the treble swivel. Tie a short trace to one eye and a longer trace to the other, matching both to, say, either a size 8 or 10 freshwater hook. You can now bait up with whatever you fancy and cast out. The diagram on page 81 should make the tackle clear but be careful not to whack the float into the wall if you can help it. They are very useful, but they are made of plastic after all. If you treat them properly you will not have any problems, but do be aware that they will not stand the same

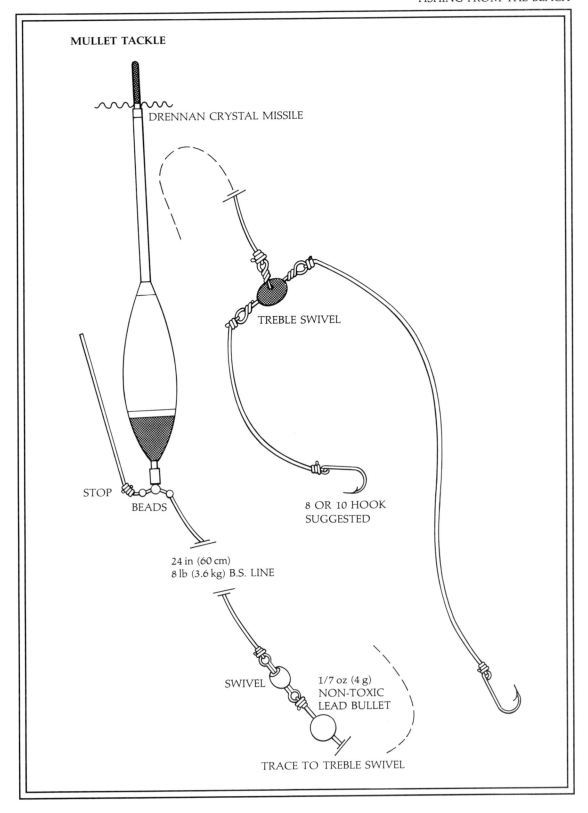

MULLET TACKLE

DRENNAN CRYSTAL MISSILE

TREBLE SWIVEL

8 OR 10 HOOK
SUGGESTED

STOP

BEADS

24 in (60 cm)
8 lb (3.6 kg) B.S. LINE

SWIVEL

1/7 oz (4 g)
NON-TOXIC
LEAD BULLET

TRACE TO TREBLE SWIVEL

sort of rough treatment that sea-fishing floats are traditionally made to withstand.

Another point to bear in mind is the position of your local beach in relation to any tidal rivers in your area. In late autumn the flounders living in your local estuaries will begin their trek to their spawning grounds, moving ahead of any sudden rushes of fresh water caused by prolonged rainfall. From the mouth of the estuary they will spread out and may then be caught in reasonable numbers from any beach that stands upon their migratory route, accepting razorfish, ragworm, lugworm, mussels, silver ragworm and, that flounder bait *par excellence*, peeler crab, with gusto. Some anglers will slide coloured beads on their traces – red, white, orange or yellow – or other attractors, such as tiny metal spoons which you can buy in packets of ten, while others will claim these make no difference whatsoever. I think they do seem to work but would stress that the most important points to remember are choosing a good bait and making sure the bait does not fall off the hook during the cast.

Peeler crab, with or without attractors, is probably the favourite bait for flatfish in my region, but this may be different where you live. Have a word with other local anglers and see what they say. If you do find yourself using peeler crab, it will pay you to get yourself some of the very fine shirring elastic

School bass will put up a very good fight on light tackle, but please return any that are smaller than 18 in (45 cm) as quickly as possible.

that is now popular with match anglers. It is useful for securing the body and is so fine you need not worry about knotting it.

To bait with peeler crab, start by peeling the claws and threading them up the shank of a 1/0 Aberdeen and onto the trace. Peel the body of the crab but leave one of the back leg sockets to provide an anchorage point for the hook. If it is a big peeler, it will pay you to cut it in half and thread only one half of the body onto the hook, passing the point through the back, turning it and then passing it out of the leg socket. Whip it on securely with the elastic and finish by peeling two or three legs and hooking them so that they trail from the bend of the hook. This should sort out any flounders (or plaice) in the region of your tackle but will also attract the attention of the crabs. If they become too much of a problem then slide a buoyancy aid — tiny floats which you can buy from tackle shops — onto your trace, together with a bead and stop, and set the float so that it is at least 6 in (150 mm) away from your bait.

One last tactic which is worth trying is to present a soft-backed crab on a hair rig to a size 2 Aberdeen. This will not only tempt flounders, but is also a deadly tactic for bass, especially if you are fishing near a pier or breakwater in the late autumn. At this time of the year you will often find bass and flounders swimming very close together, and both will go for the softback with a great deal of enthusiasm. It is also worth trying in the summer, when you may tempt the occasional smooth-hound, particularly if you live in the Dorset area. These will give a terrific fight on light tackle which is, after all, far more interesting than bullying them ashore on a beachcaster.

Generally, once you have explored your local beach thoroughly, you should find that the lighter the tackle you use, the more fun you will have, and this applies just as much to beaches as to headlands or piers. All right, perhaps on some nights you will only catch whiting, but on a beachcaster these smaller fish have little chance to do anything other than be simply winched ashore. Get those same whiting on a carp rod, which has a range of up to 90 yd (80 m) and you will find that even they can put up a struggle. There is far more to fishing a beach than simply aiming at the horizon and hurtling your lead as far out to sea as you can. If you don't believe me then why not experiment and see for yourself? You may very well be quite pleasantly surprised.

CHAPTER SIX

ESTUARIES AND NATURAL HARBOURS

Early-morning sunlight filtered through the shallow water, casting its strange luminescence over the frantic world that raced beneath. Seaweed drifted by or swirled in the grip of the currents, casting shadows that occasionally scattered the creatures over which they were passing; strange, distorted shadows which were also, for the most part, ignored. Familiarity breeds contempt, although the denizens of this undersea world are all too familiar with the concept of danger coming from above, as was evident when the swift shape of a cormorant, gliding through the surface and surging forward with powerful strokes of its wings, sent them all scurrying for cover. Then, when the danger was past, they emerged cautiously to look around or seize on whatever morsels they could find.

At the point, where the tide was racing in earnest, the shoals of mackerel chasing sand-eels were suddenly disturbed by an impact on the surface. For a moment they scattered, but when they returned it was to chase a delicate silver shape that fluttered enticingly before them, leading ever closer to the shallows. For a moment it looked as if the leader would close, but then, at the last moment, its attention was diverted and the silvery shape was drawn from the water and out of their sight.

Just past the point, where the currents settled in an eddy, a flounder suddenly shook itself free of the sand and turned hungrily around. A faint smell distracted it, so it expanded its gills and passed as much water over them as it could, sending it over sensory organs tuned to identify both scent and the direction from where it came. Now, very faintly, it caught the distinct fragrance of a peeler crab; more than that, this one seemed to be injured or perhaps even recently dead. Curious, hungry, it glided over the bottom in pursuit of the smell.

Nor was it alone. Around it, it could see the hunting shapes of bass — fierce, merciless predators — except this time, fortunately, too small to disturb or distract it. Instead, becoming steadily more emboldened as the smell intensified, the flounder gathered speed as it came closer to its intended meal. Then, just as it was about to leave the relative tranquillity of the eddy, it came into sight of its prey. Curious, tempted, it settled down for a moment before drawing close.

It was a crab, it decided. The smell was so strong it could almost, indeed could, taste the juices flowing freely from the carcass, but near it were other objects, strange and compelling, which aroused its curiosity. A silvery shape, half-buried in the sand. No danger from that. It looked at the other objects, too small to be dangerous, their colour exciting it further. No, there was no danger here. Satisfied it drew closer, nibbled on the crab and then bolted it down before anything else could tear it away.

Content, pausing only to make sure that it had not been spotted, the flounder stayed where it was for a few seconds and then began to swim strongly away.

Moments later it knew that something was terribly wrong. An invisible force was pulling it towards the shallows, away from the safety of the deeper water. Galvanized, it sped forward, resisting the pull as, with powerful strokes of its tail, it surged away from the shore.

Back on the sand the angler turned the rod to exert side-strain on the fish, letting out line reluctantly from the drag under a pressure which the flounder could not maintain for long. For a few seconds the tip was pulled round, but then the angler moved it away, checking the spool with his finger while the fish found itself following the lead and being drawn closer to where the angler was waiting. For a moment it was visible, but then it turned again and drove itself away with great slaps of the tail. The angler was once again forced to give line but this time, as before, he controlled its flight and again drew it closer. This time there were no last-minute lunges, so the flounder found itself enveloped in mesh and drawn swiftly from the water. There was to be no escape.

* * *

On this particular morning I was fishing near the point of the River Teign, where the estuary gives into the sea. It is a beautiful spot, but can be difficult to fish because of the strength of the currents and the amount of seaweed that is caught by them. It is, however, especially in the early morning when boat traffic is minimal, richly endowed with marine life, particularly sandeels, which are the prey of bass, flatfish, mackerel and garfish. By and large, when the tide is at its strongest, the flounders lie low while the bass and mackerel forage for food. Then, as the tide eases, so the flounders emerge, taking advantage of any eddies or the shallows where they can feed in relative safety. Eels drift past in large numbers,

A specimen flounder taken from the River Teign.

scooping up injured sandeels while, here and there, leaping clear of the water, the occasional salmon begins the last stage of its trek back from the sea. There are also mullet and crabs in profusion.

How you fish the mark will depend on what you want to catch. If you are interested in flatfish, you can experiment by casting into

On some days you can have great fun with school bass on the fly, but please put them back if they are under 3 lb (1.4 kg).

the eddies, but, by and large, you would do better to leave the point completely and move further up the estuary, especially in the summer when they will penetrate quite far inland. At the point, and generally on any estuary where there are sandbanks in or near the mouth (which is to say most if not all of them), it seems a pity not to try for the bass. Certainly you can get some very interesting sport, and float-fished live sandeels are a killing method which will also take mackerel.

It is also a mark where you can experiment with fly-fishing tackle. Bass, like mackerel, will take the larger flies quite readily but, if they are not in an obliging mood, you can very often change their minds by switching the fly to a small rubber eel, such as a Redgill, Westender or Eddystone eel. If there is a bit of wind, you can even counter this by changing to one of the small lead-headed eels that are now available. These are particularly useful for coalfish, mackerel and pollack. Then, when you finally connect with a fish, you will find that the fight from even a small bass is terrific.

The price of your outfit will obviously depend on your pocket, with reels varying in price from under £10 to well over £100. A cheap and cheerful one to begin with might be the Masterline Sportsman from Ryobi, which is well under £10 and will at least enable you to determine whether you are going to like the sport, after which you can always step up to a more expensive reel if you wish. If you want a better reel to begin with, without going mad, then have a look at the Ryobi 455. I found it easy to get on with and a pleasure to use. It is also not too hard on the pocket, retailing at under £25 at the time of writing.

You will also find a similar difference in the price of rods. Now, if you only intend to get a little bit of use from the outfit, shop around and see what you can pick up. If, however, the idea has a lot of appeal, then why not treat yourself to something nice to begin with? Certainly it will pay you in terms of the distance you can reach. When I started I bought a fairly basic 9 ft (2·74 m) rod, but

High summer can be a great time to go after bass, especially when they are shoaling at the mouths of estuaries.

quickly outgrew the limitations which this imposed, especially if I came into contact with larger fish. Now I use a Ryobi Challenge – the 10 ft 6 in (3·2 m) model – which gives me more distance and allows me to exercise greater control over any fish that I catch. Whichever rod takes your fancy, I would strongly advise you to make sure that you do not drop below 10 ft (3 m) in length. If you go much shorter than this, you may well find the outfit lacks sensitivity and, generally, is not very nice to fish with.

Once you have bought your outfit, you will find that there are several occasions when you can put it to very good use. Some of the most spectacular sport I have ever experienced came when a shoal of mackerel trapped a huge shoal of fry between the sand and themselves. They were not interested in natural baits, but tiny spinners and flashy silver flies made a killing. Also, as they were only a few feet out from the shore, distance was no problem. The only real danger came from making sure that you did not hook any of the other anglers! It was super sport and it is a scene which is repeated virtually every summer at the beginning of the season. Go down in the early morning when the shoals are in a feeding frenzy such as this and the chances are that it will be a session you will never forget.

However, before you start learning how to cast, you will need to get your fly line sorted out. This can be a real pain, so I was very glad when Ryobi brought out their Challenge fly lines, factory-joined to backing line and with a leader loop already in position. As an added bonus it also came in a neat little fly box, which I thought was a very good idea. Just reel it on and get on with it with a minimum of fuss. The only thing you need do is to take a length of nylon and attach it to the leader loop, which I did by taking a 7 ft (2 m) length of 9 lb (4 kg) breaking-strain nylon, tying a blood-bight loop and then attaching this to the leader knot. You can do this very simply by pushing the loop through the leader, taking the end of the nylon and passing this through the loop. Pull on the end until the whole length has passed through the loop and it will finally bed down nice and tightly, but with the added advantage of still being able to be changed. There is no knot to cut.

When you are ready to cast, first make sure that there is no one else around. On the occasions when I first tried an outfit I felt a bit of a wally, so I deliberately chose times when it was unlikely that other people would be around. Early mornings seemed to be ideal, especially those lovely mornings when the air is still and you can concentrate on what you are doing and know there is a good chance of catching fish. I found it a very relaxing method, just casting out, letting the fly be drawn away and then retrieving it slowly in little spurts, feeding the line through the fingers of my left hand while the right hand did the pulling. It was very enjoyable.

To cast the fly you will need to practise over water, rather than trying over grass. Fly line is expensive and the last thing you want to do is to abrade the line and shorten its life. Once you find a good place to practise, start by pulling a length of line from the reel and laying it in tidy coils. Hold the rod in front of you, say at roughly the 2 o'clock position, with the line held in your left hand at roughly waist height, and then briskly sweep the rod up to the 12 o'clock position, giving it a backwards flick to take it back to 11 o'clock. When the line is fully extended behind you, push the rod back to 2 o'clock so that it begins to travel back in front of you. As the fly starts to settle on the water, so you can lower the rod tip into a more comfortable position.

It may seem complicated, but in essence all you are doing is imitating the movements of someone cracking a whip. You can see this for yourself if you look at the sequence of diagrams on page 89. Then, as you become more confident, you can increase your distance by feeding the line between the fingers of your left hand during the initial stages of the cast. Gradually you will find your movements becoming more fluid and your results more

FLY-CASTING

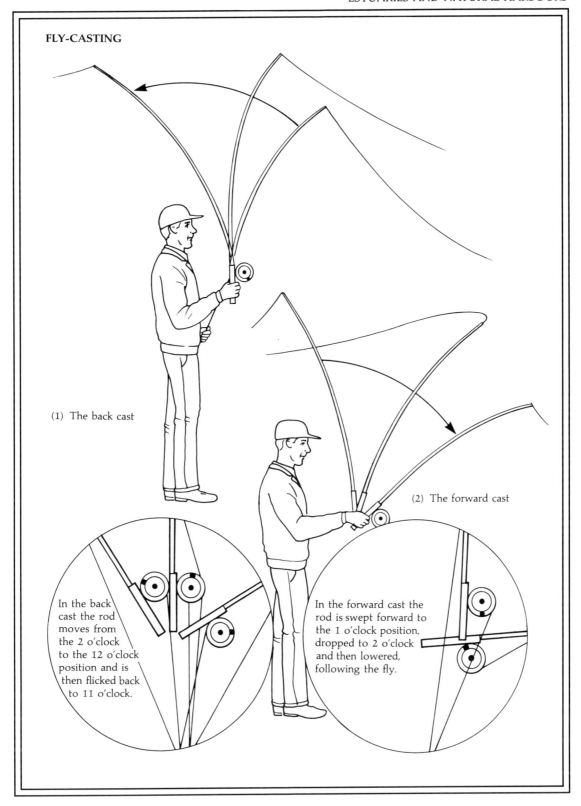

(1) The back cast

(2) The forward cast

In the back cast the rod moves from the 2 o'clock to the 12 o'clock position and is then flicked back to 11 o'clock.

In the forward cast the rod is swept forward to the 1 o'clock position, dropped to 2 o'clock and then lowered, following the fly.

creditable, until you begin to really enjoy what you are doing. It certainly grows on you, especially after you have landed a decent fish or two.

Fly-fishing is enjoyable, but it is not everybody's cup of tea. Spinning with a carp rod across the estuary mouth can also give some good results, especially if you experiment with Cebar lures or Redgills. Another popular method is float-fishing, particularly if you use self-weighted floats matched only to a swivel, trace and live sand-eel on a 1/0 hook. The crucial factor is the sandeel, which is the natural bait that fish expect to find at locations such as this. You can hook them in several ways, but the most popular seem to be either nicking a piece of skin at the back of the head,

just behind the eyes, or passing the hook through the mouth, out of the gills and then lightly nicking the flesh of the stomach. Set the float to fish at roughly the same depth as the water in front of you and then cast it out. The current will get hold of it and the sandeel, without a weight nearby to impede its natural swimming motion, will be swept along in its grip until either you retrieve it or it is attacked by a predator.

I mentioned earlier that flounders move upstream in the summer. Well, the same is true of mullet, which will often travel quite long distances from the mouth of the estuary. When you locate a shoal, move a little way above them and anchor some bread in the neighbourhood by tying it to a piece of line

Mullet can be caught from rocks near the entrance or from marks further up the estuary itself.

and then throwing it out, making sure you can recover the line later. With luck, the mullet will move upstream to find it, especially if you judiciously put in a little loose feed, and, once they are there, you can trot your float tackle down to meet them, baiting your hook with bread, worm, sweetcorn or whatever your local favourite is. If you catch one, try to move it away without spooking the rest of the shoal. That way you can usually manage to take more than one before the shoal realizes that something is up.

Another great thing about estuaries is the way in which sport flourishes at times when perhaps other areas are not fishing very well, particularly in the south of England, where the numbers of cod are trivial compared with the numbers up north. Here, when the winter draws in and we find ourselves relegated to dogfish or whiting, so the flounders begin to trek down the rivers, making their way out to sea, where any number of anglers are waiting for them with leger or paternoster tackle. Take, for example, the River Teign in Devon, which is quite justly famed for its flounders, producing some very big specimens with a fair sprinkling of 4 lb (1·8 kg) fish among them. Consequently, when my friend Charles asked me if I was interested in entering a roving competition on the Teign, I decided to take him to the docks where we would have easy access for his wheelchair and still have a good chance of catching a reasonable fish. In hindsight, that may have been a mistake.

Another occurred almost immediately after we started fishing. I was re-baiting Charles' hook with peeler crab when a group of swans — about 30 strong — decided suddenly to change direction and all took off at once. I jumped up to grab my rod but, before I could reach it, one of them collided with the line and that took off as well, taking with it the tripod on which it was resting. The reel hit the side of the quay and the whole outfit disappeared over the side, where it now set off in the direction in which the swan was swimming.

Fortunately for me there were several anglers fishing alongside us. They very kindly cast over the rod and managed to get it back, where we now found that it was attached to a very angry swan! I tried to guide it to the shore as gently as I could, but at that moment it managed to free itself, leaving only a small clump of down in its place. I reeled-in and examined the mess it had made of my reel, a brand-new ABU 6500 which I was using for only the second time that morning.

After this incident, I was really regretting my choice of venue. Add the fact that it was now blowing a gale and I think you can see why. Still, I thought, naïvely, to myself: 'What else can go wrong?' I should have known that was tempting fate!

The next incident started quite innocently. Charles went off for a short walk on his crutches. I continued to fish but when, 10 minutes later, there was no sign of his return, I began to get worried, especially as such a length of time on his feet takes a great deal of effort, as other multiple-sclerosis sufferers will realize. Another 5 minutes passed and this time I decided to take his wheelchair and find him. It was a good intention and unfortunately went the way of so many others.

I took the brakes off the chair and turned it round, then reached down to put Charles' bag on his coat to stop it blowing away. The next second an enormous gust of wind surged up behind the chair and sent it spinning away. I dropped the bag and ran after it, to the hilarity of other anglers who shouted at the sight of me pelting down the docks after a runaway wheelchair! I ran as fast as I could but, before I could reach it, it hurtled over the side and disappeared in seconds. Only a faint stream of bubbles gave any indication of where it had come to rest at the bottom of the docks.

'Oh bother!' I thought and, if you believe that, then you probably still believe in the tooth fairy! However, once again my fellow anglers came to my rescue and between us we were able to retrieve the chair, just in time for

A late-autumn flounder in super condition.

Peeler crabs are the number-one bait for flounders in the River Teign. They have a similar attraction for many other species.

Charles to witness some ten or so anglers pulling on a motley collection of rope to which was now attached his wheelchair, unfortunately minus its arms. He looked mildly surprised, but was quite unperturbed when we dragged it ashore, simply taking a teacloth and wiping it down before sitting on it and carrying on fishing as if nothing had happened.

Nothing else did happen for a while after that, but then his rod, a medium-weight telescopic, set up with running leger and a whole peeler crab to a 2/0 hook, gave a series of twitches. At the first one he gave it slack but then, as the bites got more decisive, he swept the rod up and bent into the fish. This hurtled away, putting a satisfying bend in the rod, but Charles controlled it and brought it closer to the docks where we could see that it was a very nice flounder. Once again it dived towards the bottom, as it did several times, but eventually Charles lifted it out of the water and we were able to bring it ashore, handlining it up the side of the docks where we could finally weigh it. A lovely autumn flounder in prime condition weighing just under $2\frac{3}{4}$ lb (1·2 kg), Charles' first flounder, typical of the Teign and a specimen which went on to win him a Christmas hamper.

Flounders are very obliging fish. There are great nights when the crabs are put down by the frosts and the flounders have a heyday in their absence. This is just as much true of natural harbours, such as Poole in Dorset, as it is of estuaries. In both cases you can fish for them and, indeed, any of the species I have mentioned in this chapter in exactly the same way.

There is, however, one method which I really ought to mention before leaving the subject of flounders and that is the baited spoon. This is a method, devised many years ago by Mr J. P. Gerrard, which consists of a large spoon being trolled slowly along the bottom with the current. Attached to the spoon by a short trace is a baited hook, giving the tackle its name of 'baited spoon'. It is, quite frankly, a method which works well when it is used properly, but over the years I have heard and seen many people rubbish the method when they have not even been using it correctly to begin with. If you are thinking of using it then there are a few points which you should bear in mind: the tackle works best of all from a boat, for which it was originally designed, and it must be worked with the current, not against it. Now that is easy enough to arrange from a boat, but from shore that means the best places to use it will be bridges over estuaries or natural harbours. Here you can cast out against the current and then retrieve the tackle with it, taking care that you do not reel in too fast and that you stop immediately you feel a bite, pulling a good 'four-foot yard' from the spool. As you reel in so you will discover that the spoon imparts to the rod a steady rhythmic motion, like the tick-tock of an old grandfather clock. If you get a faster rhythm then you are reeling too fast. Slow down and let the spoon sink back nearer the bottom.

You do exactly the same thing if you go afloat in a dinghy. The only difference is that, instead of reeling in, you will be drifting with the current or pottering along with the engine. You can also get away with using much lighter rods and reels, perhaps scaling down to a trigger-grip baitcaster matched with a light multiplier such as the ABU Ambassadeur Maxxar or the Ryobi T20. If you get a bite you will find yourself with a spectacular fight on your hands and that, for me, is what fishing with light tackle is all about.

CHAPTER SEVEN

PIER FISHING AT NIGHT

The light of three Tilley lamps twinkled in the crisp chill of the winter evening, while several anglers moved from rod to rod, casting, baiting their hooks or just talking. Others stood waiting, watching little red lights that broke the darkness and could be seen from the end of the pier, moving slightly in the faint breeze that barely ruffled the water. It was a tranquil scene, but there was also an air, a feeling of excitement, running from the oldest present to the youngest, that perhaps this particular night was going to be the one for which we had been waiting all week.

One of the anglers suddenly leapt for his rod, while the rest of us simply nodded at the telltale rattle, the characteristic trademark of a small whiting. Curious eyes watched for a moment longer, until we saw the fish break surface, then the usual banter began. 'That your bait, Michael?' asked one angler, his comment matched by others, less printable, from the other anglers nearby. The question was answered with a grin and a shake of the head, while the rest of us chuckled over some of the fruitier comments. On a pier such as this you get a lot of well-natured ribbing, so you get used to unhooking and returning any smaller fish as gently and quickly as possible.

For a while nothing happened, then the carp rod off the end of the pier gave a decided lunge, the tip being pulled down in a series of bites that were so determined that the butt of the rod was momentarily lifted from the floor. 'Whose is this...?' cried one angler, but Anthony was already there, striking upwards

and into the fish at the other end. 'I'm on,' he cried, struggling to hold the rod up. 'No, you're not, are you?' came back the sarcastic response, the angler concerned looking pointedly at the way the rod was bent nearly double. The rest of us grinned and crowded around.

The end of the rod nodded, then bent over hard so that Anthony was forced to pump the fish upwards, until it was once more near the surface, where he fought to keep it, keeping it as high as possible to avoid the weed and rocks that lay at the base of the pier. Once again the tip was pulled down as the fish gave another decisive dive, this time taking line from the drag before it could be brought under control. 'Get the rod up!' we shouted. 'Don't let it get near the bottom.'

For a couple of minutes it looked as though the fish was going to find cover, but then Anthony managed to get it back up to the surface, where it ran rather than dived. Moments later it was brought to the side of the pier and then landed, a typical dogfish weighing just under 2 lb (0·9 kg), not a specimen but a reasonable fish for this particular mark. 'Is that it?' asked one angler. 'The way your rod was going I thought you had a bull huss or at least something decent!'

Both of us grinned, as we have met this reaction so many times over the years. The main species from this mark — Babbacombe Pier in South Devon — are dogfish, whiting and pout on the bottom, or, during the summer, mackerel, garfish, wrasse, pollack, scad or

Dogfish are an obliging species that fight well on light tackle and are quite easy to catch.

mullet on float. There are other species, of course — I have caught rockling, bull huss, conger, rays and flatfish on the odd occasion — but these are few and far between. By far the greatest number of fish caught on the bottom are dogfish and whiting, for which carp rods such as the Ryobi John Wilson or Normark Pro Specialist Carp are ideal. These have the length and the power necessary to deal with any larger fish — should they come along — and can put a 2 oz (57 g) lead weight 100 yd (90 m) out if it is needed. (Please bear in mind, however, that this distance is unlikely to be required on a large number of the piers that you are likely to visit.) They are also sufficiently sensitive for you to get a very good fight from any smaller fish that come along.

On the subject of the distance that you need to cast, one thing I have noticed is that people seem to forget that fish are drawn to piers because of the populations of crabs, prawns and smaller fish that they support, most of which will be hiding or foraging for food very close to the pier itself. They are, if you like, the main attraction! Now this applies not only to the actual pier, but also to any underwater obstacles in its vicinity. All of these creatures feel a bit more confident with a spot of cover about them, so they tend to take refuge in whatever underwater foliage is closest to hand. Predators, naturally, are aware of this, so they browse around the areas where they know there is a good chance of a meal. Sooner or later this is noticed by anglers and the next thing you hear is that such and such a person found a real hot spot on a particular trip. Word gets around and you soon find that people are concentrating on these spots to the exclusion of other areas. Each angler has his or her own 'favourite' spot. Now sometimes these hot spots can be right at the base of the pier or sometimes they can be a bit further out but, if they are 20 yd (18 m) out and you cast 100 yd (90 m), you will totally miss the very fish that you want to catch. You should try and fish as near to them as possible, or at least put your tackle where you might intercept any

fish that are travelling between them. I would stress, however, the *near* in the last sentence. If you cast directly into these very snaggy areas, the chances are that you will lose your tackle.

Another point to bear in mind is that there are, on many piers, numerous underwater obstructions which claim a lot of tackle. Now during the day this is less of a problem because you can see where they are, particularly at low tide. Therefore it makes sense to visit the pier during daylight hours and try to map out their position for future reference. This will save you plenty of gear and help to identify where the best spots are likely to be. You should also try to find out what the bottom is like. If it is rocks giving way to sand, then very often the best spot to fish will be right at the edge of the sand, where predators can surprise any creatures that emerge from cover. The closer you get to the rocks the more fish you will catch, although the chances are that, on occasion, you may lose both the fish and your tackle to boot.

Casting a little bit further will place your bait in a good position to intercept any predators, while simultaneously reducing the amount of tackle that you are likely to lose. Another tactic is to put a lead lift above your weight. When you reel-in, the pressure from the water makes this act like a kite, so that it glides towards the surface and lifts your tackle over the obstructions. Once you have discovered where the fish are lying, why not place a loop of line behind the spool clip on your reel and cast — as gently as possible — to the same spot every time. If you have no spool clip on your reel, then cast to where you think the fish are, take the spool off and lock the line at the right place with a rubber band. This will stop any future casts so that you are fishing the same spot every time, laying up a very strong scent trail to draw fish to your bait.

This is actually a very good tactic. Once the fish in the area 'get wind', so to speak, of your bait, then they will home-in until they find it. If you keep going back to the same spot, you

Dogfish, whiting and mackerel, all taken on double leger on a particularly hard night.

should find that you do quite well, particularly if you use a strong-smelling attractor, such as peeler crab, squid or fresh mackerel. If you want cod, change your bait to either a whole *calamari* squid or several black lug.

As to terminal tackle, well, everybody has their own ideas for their end rigs, but for pier-fishing I would stick to running leger. If you use a double leger, set up 'wishbone style' as illustrated on page 99, and stick on two 1/0 Aberdeens for the hooks, you should do reasonably well. If you use peeler crabs for bait, you will find that they will tempt bass, dogfish, flatfish, rays, whiting and cod, depending on the season, while two large pieces of squid – say half the body of a

calamari squid on each hook – will take reasonable whiting as well as dogfish – both lesser and greater spotted – cod, rays, rockling and bass. On the odd occasion I have also caught mackerel on the bottom, although these seem to go for strips rather than chunks.

To set up a double leger, start by tying a leader to your main line to take the initial shock of casting. This is important as even a light rod can throw out a 2 oz (57 g) lead weight with sufficient force to cause a lot of injury. If you have a snap-off, you could do someone a serious mischief. You must bear in mind that your main line will be much lighter than usual (I use either 8 or 10 lb/3·6 or 4·5 kg breaking strain for this type of fishing) and it is

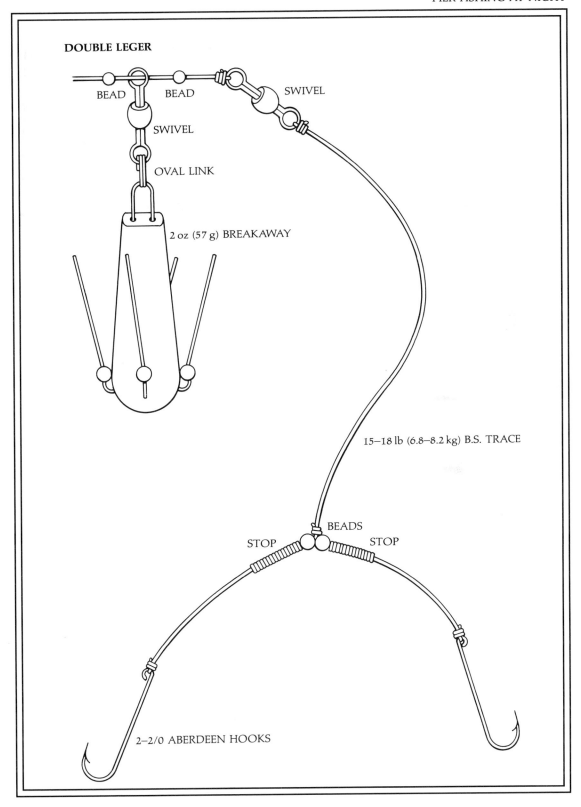

DOUBLE LEGER

BEAD   BEAD   SWIVEL

SWIVEL

OVAL LINK

2 oz (57 g) BREAKAWAY

15–18 lb (6.8–8.2 kg) B.S. TRACE

BEADS

STOP   STOP

2–2/0 ABERDEEN HOOKS

therefore very easy to break. However, because you will not be casting more than a 2 oz (57 g) lead weight, you will only need a leader of, say, 25 lb (11·3 kg) breaking-strain line, perhaps twice the length of your rod. Tie this on with a leader knot and you are ready to start on the rest of your rig.

Which leader knot you use is up to you, but on page 101 I have illustrated a good one that you might like to experiment with. This is very strong and recommended by anglers who are heavily involved with tournament casting. The other things that you will need to make for the tackle are a blood-bight loop — illustrated on page 77 — and some telephone-wire stops.

To put the tackle together you run a bead, swivel and bead onto your leader, then tie a swivel to the end. Clip a weight to the first swivel with either a split ring or oval link and then cut a length of trace for your hooks. What breaking strain is up to you, but whiting have fairly sharp teeth and, if there are a lot of them around, they will make short work of the lighter lines. I would suggest upping your trace to 18 lb (8·2 kg) breaking strain, perhaps even 25 lb (11·3 kg). Tie a hook to one end and then slide on a stop, bead, another bead and stop, in that order; then tie a second hook to the end of the trace. Lay the two hooks beside each other, each with a stop and a bead, and then tie a blood bight so that you end up with a large loop on one side and the two hooks dangling off the knot. Cut one side of the loop and tie it to the second swivel. Tighten the stops and then pull the line tight, sliding them up so that they trap the beads against the knot. Each of the beads is trapped against the other so that the hook snoods are forced apart, making this a very difficult tackle to tangle. The diagram should make this clear.

Another useful tactic is float-fishing, where the float comes complete with a transparent tube into which you can insert a Starlite. These are brilliant for night-fishing and have all the advantages of float-fishing during the day, namely that they will lift your bait over any obstructions and into the view of any predators. They are also very versatile, taking pollack or whiting on live prawns, shrimps or mackerel strip, bass on live sandeels or prawns, and mackerel on mackerel strip or live sandeels. They will also take scad in the summer.

There are three other points which you should bear in mind when you consider fishing from a pier, especially if you intend to go late at night: making sure that you have some sort of light close to hand, warm clothing, and landing the fish. If there is a light, then landing any fish, or indeed any operation, is made that much simpler. If, however, there are no lights where you are fishing, you will need to provide some of your own. There are a variety of torches available but probably the most useful to have a look at are headlamps, such as the Petzl Zoom. These are very robust, comfortable and efficient. They can also be quickly converted to take four rechargeable batteries, which is a lot cheaper on your pocket and more environmentally friendly than using standard batteries. Just take a trip to your local electrical bits-and-pieces store and you can buy a four-battery holder for well under £1. Hook it up with a couple of spade-end clips and you are in business. The four rechargeables will give you plenty of light and last for several hours. When you are finished just plug them into the recharging unit and a few hours later they will be ready to use again.

Another useful addition is a lantern. Personally, I like the Coleman lamps, especially the unleaded models, but there are quite a few others on the market which are well worth investigating. You might even like to look at some of the electric models which are available. These are a cross between a torch and a lamp and, while they are not as bright as some Tilley lamps, there is no possibility of your transferring any lingering smell of petrol to your bait.

Lanterns and headlamps are both very useful, but even with them it can be very hard spotting bites. Now, you can make it easier by

SHOCK LEADER KNOT

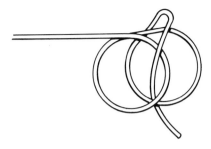

(1) Taking the heavier line first, make two loops around your finger and then slide them off. Pass the end in and out of both loops.

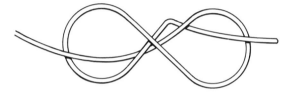

(2) Pass one loop through the other, then slowly tighten them until they form a figure-of-eight knot with two spaces through which to pass the lighter line.

(3) Pass the lighter line through one of the spaces and then out of the other. Wrap it around the heavier line six times, then pass it back through the first twist and through the figure-of-eight in the opposite direction, back the way it came.

(4) Pull tight on both strands evenly, lubricating the knot as you tighten it so that it beds down into a small compact knot. Trim off the protruding ends. Any stress is now on the heavier rather than the lighter line.

wrapping the rod tip with reflective tape or painting it with luminous paint, but a useful accessory, which is well worth investing in, is a tip light. These operate from a couple of 675 watch batteries and are visible from a considerable distance. They are invaluable for legering and give off a bright red light which makes bite detection so much easier than straining your eyes in the effort to pick out the rod tip on the edges of your vision. They are not very expensive, certainly under £5, and they do last a long time. When they run out, just replace the batteries. The first ones I bought lasted over 80 hours before I had to replace them, so they do make a lot of sense. You might also try taping a Starlite, which is a plastic tube filled with chemicals, to the tip of the rod. You bend and shake the tube and a chemical reaction starts which gives off a reasonable light. Each tube lasts for some 8–10 hours and, if you go home early, you can stop the reaction by popping the Starlite in the freezer until you need it again. Then just take it out the next time you go fishing, give it a shake and pop it on your rod.

Warm clothing is another must for night-fishing. Thermal suits are probably the best answer, with both inner and outer suits available, but they can be a bit expensive. If you put on an inner suit over a T-shirt, with a jumper and outer thermal over the top, you will usually find that you can be comfortable on even the worst of nights, although you will need to make sure that your hands and head are covered. Mittens are a good idea because they leave the tips of your fingers free for tying any fiddly knots, while deerstalkers or even the old bobble hats are ideal for keeping your head warm.

Lastly, if you catch a decent fish you will need either a drop net or landing net to get it ashore. A drop net will take care of any places where there are no steps close to hand, but it is awkward for tackling anything really decent, especially in the dark where it is difficult to see. If there are steps nearby, then a landing net is a better answer, but you do need to be careful. If you are the only person fishing and you slip into the water, you will find yourself in a very dangerous position, especially in the winter if you are wearing cold-weather gear. This can quickly become waterlogged and weigh you down so do, please, take care. Better yet, take a friend who can net the fish for you. That way there is someone nearby if you run into difficulties and it really does make things a lot simpler than trying to manage steps, net, rod and fish on your own. Piers are, after all, ideal places to fish with either one or several friends, but they should also be treated with respect. They do give way into fairly deep water and there are often fairly strong currents around them. Have fun while you are fishing, but keep safety firmly in mind, especially on slippery steps with an unpredictable swell. It will certainly pay you to do so. Night-fishing from a pier has a special charm that makes it, on a good night, thoroughly entertaining. I hope you enjoy it as much as I do.

CHAPTER EIGHT

GETTING AFLOAT

Like most other anglers, I have longed for a high-powered craft that will take me miles out to sea, only to come face to face with the same reality that confronts every other would-be boat angler, namely the expense. Add up the total cost of the boat, engine, mooring fees, maintenance and extras such as safety equipment and you will soon find that the sheer cost of the project makes it prohibitive for many people. Include the difficulty of actually finding a convenient mooring in the first place – which is hard when the area in which you live is oversubscribed – and you can see that it is not only expensive, but will also take very careful planning to realize.

So what are the options? One might be to pool resources with a friend and share the expense, but for that you need a very sound friendship and a solvent partner. If either of you lose your job, for whatever reason, then the pressure upon the partner who is employed becomes intense and may even put a strain upon your relationship. Another might be simply to hire a boat when you want to, but the trouble with that is the hire rates tend to be expensive and very often the boat can only potter along. Such boats also tend to be bottom-of-the-market models which wallow in the water and are too cramped for you to really enjoy your day. The option which I preferred was to look at boats which were small enough to trail and launch, but which were also reasonably quick if I needed to get ashore in a hurry. Another point to consider was that, if the boat was light enough to be kept in my garden, I would have no storage or mooring fees to worry about.

Consequently, after examining a lot of small dinghies, I decided to investigate inflatables and opted for a Humber rigid inflatable with a 20 horsepower Mariner outboard on the back and a second-hand trailer. This outfit did everything I wanted but was also quite fast, which was an important consideration in case the weather changed for the worst. As for safety equipment I settled on flares, life-jackets for everybody, oars, an anchor with chain and just over 100 ft (30 m) of rope – far deeper than any mark I intended to fish – compass, hand-held radio, puncture-repair kit, aerosol foghorn, a universal socket set, pliers, screwdrivers, spare set of spark plugs and a torch. I tried to economize on the cost of the radio, buying a hand-held CB instead of a VHF, but speedily found that the range and application of the set was next to useless, although I had chosen one which I was assured had had good reviews and was considered a quality product. I ended up taking it back and saving up for a hand-held VHF radio. These may be expensive – the cheapest set I have seen to date was about £150 – but far more boat-owners have them than CBs and they are far more reliable. If you need help urgently, the chances are that you will raise it that much more quickly on a VHF than you will on a CB. That could make the difference between life and death. I also economized by not fitting lights, which would have had to work off the outboard and, considering the rare occasions when I go out at night, would have been a lot of money for nothing. Instead I bought the Kodak 5000, which is a waterproof, floating torch with a powerful beam. To test it out I tied a rope to it, turned it on and threw it into the sea off Babbacombe Pier, leaving it in the water for a couple of hours to see if it really was waterproof. It was.

By the time I had finished rigging myself out, I had gone through the better part of £2,000 and, even though this solution may not have been everybody's cup of tea, it was certainly mine. I could squeeze the family on board for a trip if I wanted, or launch it with only a friend to assist. If there were just the two of us, we also found that its speed, in calm water, was considerable, so that we ended up having to insure it as a speedboat. It is a light, convenient outfit with, let us be honest about it, a limited range. However, for a first boat it was ideal. It also became speedily apparent that inshore waters offered far more scope than I had previously suspected. Distance was not always as important as I had originally thought. Just steps away from the shore was a world of angling opportunities just waiting, begging to be explored, but it was also an area all too often neglected or ignored altogether, scarcely noticed by the flotilla of angling craft that sped on their way to more distant marks. As they flew swiftly past the moored vessels tied up to the pier, past pontoons or other marks, inaccessible from the shore, so they unwittingly missed out on a great deal of fun.

Some of the marks I visited could be reached by a child's inflatable! One such was the side of a ship tied up for a period in excess of a year. You could not fish it from the shore, but from the water you could tie up to the seaward side and have a great deal of fun, especially if you fished very close to the ship itself. I took my family there on a gloriously sunny day and we stayed until the light started to fade in the evening, just popping ashore every now and again to stretch our legs or get something to eat. We were all using trigger-grip baitcasters set up on float

tackle and matched with light multipliers and the sport we were having was terrific. Using 5–8 lb (2·3–8·2 kg) breaking-strain lines and the lightest floats we could find, we were scarcely dropping our lines over the side before one or the other of us was getting a bite, with a steady stream of mackerel and garfish being unhooked and released. Then Anthony decided to have a go on the bottom for a wrasse. I set him up with a double paternoster rig, baited him with ragworm and away he went, adding a number of wrasse to the fish that we had already caught.

This went on for a while, but then, as the light started to fade, so the wrasse went off the feed and Anthony changed to mackerel strip, bending almost instantly into first one fish and then a second. When he brought them up, we could see that they were a nice pair of scad. We released them and, from then on, Anthony was having bites at the rate, I should say, of at least one a minute. It was too much for the rest of us. The bites we had been having on float tackle had virtually stopped, so we all changed to paternoster and got in on the action, bringing aboard bream, pout, scad, pollack and nearly a sizeable cuttlefish, which we would have had for bait, if it had not released the pout it was holding just before we could get it to the net.

All in all it was an exciting day. I have absolutely no idea how many fish we caught altogether, though it was certainly several dozen at the least, but it was a lot of fun. We were literally only 20 yd (18 m) from the shore, albeit several hundred yards along the wall of the breakwater, and enjoying a quality of sport which we had not seen for several years. The size of the fish may not have been anything to write home about – the biggest was only about a couple of pounds – but on the light tackle we were using the fight that they gave was certainly something to remember.

Besides this particular spot there were several other marks that we fished close to shore. Basically we explored any feature –

Light telescopics can be really good fun when you are fishing close to shore. This was one of many that we caught on a day when we did not even move off the mooring.

rock, reef, pier, etc. – which you could reach with a boat but not from the shore. The results were quite exciting. Often we had our best catches from marks which were so close in that most other boats ignored them. Over the years they had built up a lot of cover, which attracted smaller creatures, such as prawns, shellfish and crabs, which, in their turn, drew predators to the spot. These found a good supply of food in a spot that was relatively undisturbed and consequently flourished. Then, when we visited, we found ourselves catching mackerel, garfish, wrasse, pollack, bass, mullet, bream, scad, whiting, pout, eels and coalfish with very little effort. All right,

we groundbaited for the mullet, mixing John Wilson Chub 'n' Barbel groundbait with breadcrumbs and minced pieces of mackerel, but on some marks we did not even have to do that. We also experimented with match rods and even cheap telescopics, such as the DAM Mega Telespin, which are very light and also convenient on a boat that is short of space. If we wanted larger fish, such as bass, we used the shorter carp rods, such as the Ryobi Wanderer/Stalker or the DAM Andy Little Stalking rod, which both performed well on the boat and which the children used extensively from the shore. We also found that, by sticking to the lighter tackle, it was much easier to fish and far more enjoyable than using conventional tackle, which would have been far too beefy for the average size of the fish that we were catching.

The terminal rigs that we used depended on the fish that we expected to catch. If we were after mackerel or garfish then we stuck to float tackle. For bass we used a running leger set up with a 6–10 ft (1·8–3 m) trace, baited with live sandeels or prawn, while, if we were after other species, we shortened the trace and baited with ragworm or mackerel strip. We also found that the double paternoster with which I set Anthony up was surprisingly successful for a number of species.

The main reason for this is that a paternoster used from a boat actually does what many anglers imagine, incorrectly, that it does from the shore, namely it holds the baits just off the bottom in full view of the fish. Now if you are fishing from the shore that does not happen. The weight of the line, cast and held at an angle from the beach, sinks to the bottom so that your bait or baits are presented on the bottom itself. From a boat the presentation is quite different. The hooks are held on a tight line and are literally suspended off the seabed. Just let the line down until the weight bumps on the bottom and then tighten up. Bites are usually quite decisive and can be hit very quickly. If you tie fairly short traces to the booms, you will also hook a large proportion of the bites that you strike, certainly more than you would with conventional leger. We found it a very useful tactic for a number of species, including scad, whiting, pollack, wrasse and pout.

Making up the rig is quite simple, but you will need a piece of carp tubing, cut up into pieces approximately 1 in (25 mm) long. You will also need some fairly small beads. Slide on a bead, piece of tubing, another bead and a swivel. Turn the end of the line back on itself and pass it back through the bead, tube and second bead. Slide the tube to where you want it and then wrap the end of the line around the main line several times. Hold the tube against

the central turn and pull tight, so that the tube will come to rest sticking straight out from the main line, with the swivel trapped tightly against its end. Do this with a second piece of tubing and you will have a double paternoster. The only thing you may have to watch is the weakening of the line when the dropper knots are tightened. This is a minor problem and one which is quickly solved if you make the tackle up on heavier line, which you can then connect to your main line with a swivel.

The main advantages of this tackle are that it is cheap and that the swivels are far more efficient than booms, eliminating a lot of the line twist which can be such a pain with conventional paternosters. The tubing holds the traces away from the main line and also helps to present the baits properly, making it a useful and versatile tackle. You can even avoid using knots to hold the tubing in place: just slide the second bead out of the way and then drop a spot or two of Superglue in the tubing itself. Put the bead back in place and the tackle will be secured with no need for any knots other than those connecting hook traces and weight. The diagrams on pages 107 and 108 should make the arrangement clear, but another point to consider is the way in which you connect the weight at the bottom. If there are a lot of snags you might like to consider tying it to a second swivel with a lighter breaking strain of monofilament than your main line. Then, if it gets stuck, you will only lose the weight and not any fish that you have caught.

Mullet were, if you will excuse the pun, a different kettle of fish altogether. For them we used the double-hook float rig described in Chapter 5, with baits varying from pieces of crab, to mackerel liver, bread, sweetcorn, harbour ragworm and maggots, depending on where we were fishing. If you want to try mullet-fishing for yourself, then decide on your bait by taking a look at where you intend to go and then making a sensible decision based on what you can see around you. If you are near to a marina then maggots and bread might well be your first choice, while ragworm

TUBING FOR DOUBLE PATERNOSTER

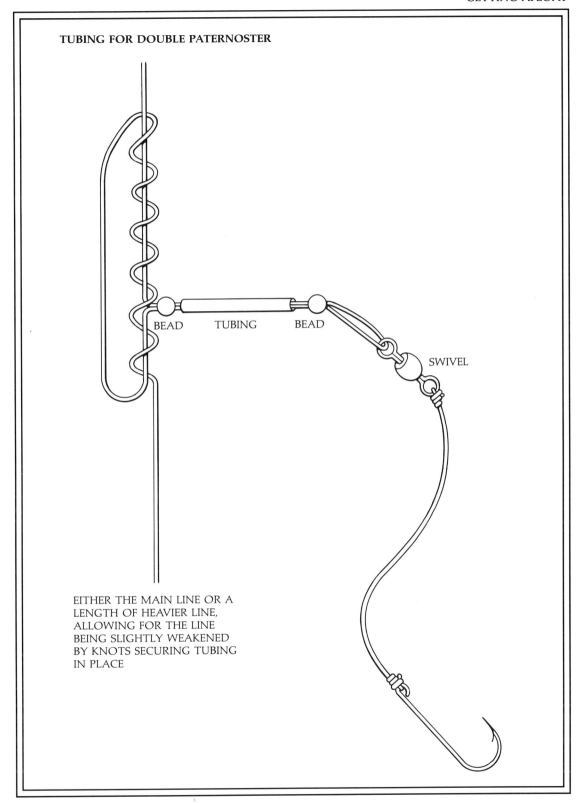

BEAD   TUBING   BEAD

SWIVEL

EITHER THE MAIN LINE OR A
LENGTH OF HEAVIER LINE,
ALLOWING FOR THE LINE
BEING SLIGHTLY WEAKENED
BY KNOTS SECURING TUBING
IN PLACE

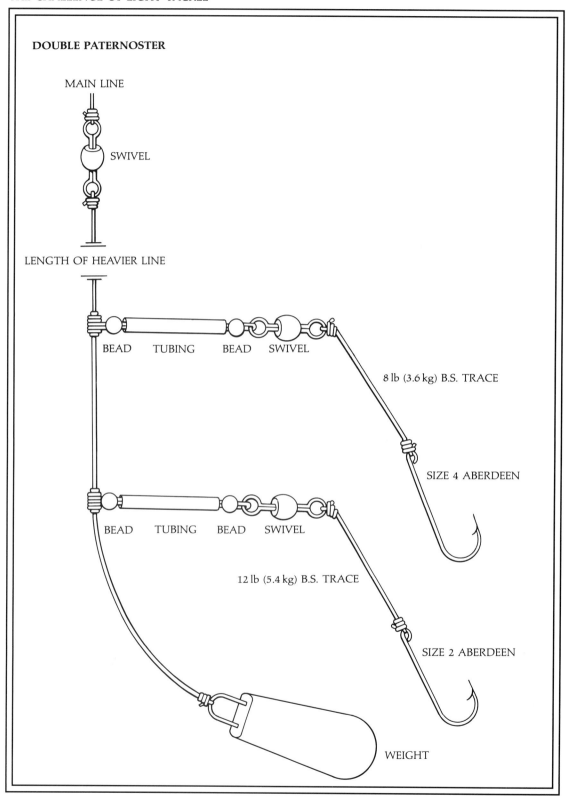

DOUBLE PATERNOSTER

MAIN LINE

SWIVEL

LENGTH OF HEAVIER LINE

BEAD   TUBING   BEAD   SWIVEL

8 lb (3.6 kg) B.S. TRACE

SIZE 4 ABERDEEN

BEAD   TUBING   BEAD   SWIVEL

12 lb (5.4 kg) B.S. TRACE

SIZE 2 ABERDEEN

WEIGHT

or small pieces of crab might be more appropriate if you are close to a secluded beach. If you are near an open beach then bread is also a good option. Sweetcorn is useful near sewage outfalls.

While on the subject of baits, an accessory which you might find useful is the excellent Flow-Troll, a livebait container which is weighted in such a way that you can place your livebait in it and then throw it overboard, even if you are moving. It is made of extremely strong and durable materials and is available from Westcountry Bait Boxes, 376 Totnes Road, Paignton, TQ4 7DG.

To use the Flow-Troll you simply push in the hinged flap and pop in your bait. Tie a rope to the handle and then throw it in the water. It automatically floats in the right position to ensure as smooth a ride as possible for its inhabitants and can then be towed at speeds of up to 8 knots. If you go over this speed then just swing the container back on board. It is designed to stay at least half-full of water so your bait should be all right for short periods of time unless, of course, you put too many in or forget to throw it back in the water when you get to your mark. If you are using live sand-eels or prawns, you would do better, when moving at speed, to empty the water out altogether and place the container away from bright sunlight. If the creatures inside get too hot, they will dry out and perish.

Another accessory which you might find useful is a rod-holder. There are always the odd times when you could do with an extra pair of hands, so it makes sense to have a permanent and secure way of holding your rod in position if you have to put it down. One I particularly liked was the Snowbee, which is very robust and well designed. I have used mine extensively throughout the season and found it extremely useful. It is well made and I thought it very good value for money.

One tactic which I would thoroughly recommend close to shore is slowly trolling a livebait along beaches and in and around coves and harbours at night. Set your engine

The Flow-Troll livebait container.

speed to as slow as you can go without stalling the engine and then potter along with as light a weight on your line as you can get away with. Non-toxic lead bullets are ideal, set to slide freely on your main line above an 8 ft (2·4 m) flowing trace. Bait up with live sand-eels and you have a very good chance of catching bass. Make sure, however, that you take at least a foghorn and a torch with you, along with a packet of spare batteries. If you are on the open sea, you will need something to signal your presence. You also need to

Jan Hutchings from Paignton with a specimen mullet.

check that you have plenty of petrol. Trolling can use up a considerable quantity of fuel and the last thing you want to do is to find yourself in the position of having to row back to the harbour from where you started out. Another point to watch is your line. I remember one particular night when a friend of mine abruptly circled to go back over a spot where he had had a likely bite. In his enthusiasm we had no chance to get our lines out of the way and they were both picked up by the propeller, stalling the engine. It took us quite a long time to sort it out, during which time the wind picked up and started blowing very strongly offshore. If we had left the anchor behind, we would have been blown a long way out before we could have been able to move under our own power again, so do please bear it in mind and watch out for your line.

While on the subject of anchors, another useful tip concerns the way in which you rig them out. I bought a folding anchor for my boat because it was both compact and heavy enough to do the job. Then, when I attached the chain, I connected it to the eye at the bottom of the anchor instead of the top. Next I laid the chain against the stem of the anchor and, using flimsy cotton, tied one of the links to the top eye. This was a tip that I had been given by a young lady named Lisa and it was very quickly justified. On one mark I dropped the anchor and it became snagged. Now, if I had attached the chain directly to the top eye, I would have been in trouble. However, instead of losing the anchor, the cotton snapped so that my pull abruptly shifted from the top of the anchor to the bottom. It was immediately dislodged and came free with no further trouble.

Besides trolling, which is a lot of fun but may be against the rules of some clubs, you might try simply drifting for bass, pollack and coalfish. Go as close to any rocks as you dare and then let the current drift you past. As you travel, so you will cover a lot of ground and, it is to be hoped, pick up a few fish. If the current

The Snowbee rod-holder is a very useful device to have on board.

is strong, you will drift quite quickly and you will need to put on a reasonable size weight, say a couple of ounces (about 60 g). If the drift is quite slow, then go as light as you can and still maintain contact with the bottom. When a bass bites it will be pretty fierce and you need to strike quickly and firmly. You may also find yourself coming up with a few surprises. The last time I tried drifting – past Thatcher's Rock in Torbay – I hooked gurnard, a sizeable wrasse and ended up with a whip conger. Still, for me, that is part of the pleasure when fishing from a boat. You have less idea of what you are going to catch than you do from the shore, which makes the fishing more exciting than ever. Add the superb fight you get from using lighter gear and you can see why, for me, getting afloat offers both a compelling and rewarding way of fishing, even if it is only yards from the shore!

CHAPTER NINE

DRIFTING OVER SANDY MARKS

There was a strange, almost eerie calm over the mist-shrouded quay, even the voices of the seagulls were muted by the drifting fog that rose, wraith-like, from the mirror surface of the water beneath. There was no sign, either on the shore or out to sea, of any person save ourselves. Instead the early morning was so still that we felt as if we were the only ones awake in the world, treading softly in a twilight dawn that someone, somewhere was dreaming.

We moved quietly, though it seemed as if every word we spoke or action we took was piercingly loud. The trailer thundered on the quay. The car engine throbbed, then roared across the water in challenge while only the boat, slipping free in its calm, unhurried manner, blended perfectly with both the mist and sea. Once again the trailer clanked and banged its way over the cobbles and then, as the car engine stuttered into silence, so the echoes fell away into the distance and died. Carefully, gently, we pulled the boat closer, stepped gingerly aboard and started to row.

As we moved away from the quay, the mist thickened slightly, then swirled to one side so we could take one final glimpse before a curtain of grey first shrouded and then hid it away. We grinned, slightly startled by the loud rustling from the bucket, then changed positions as we reached for the outboard and tugged it to life.

It came awake with a throaty roar that seemed shockingly loud, then settled into a background drone that dominated both our world and time itself; for time stood still, or so it seemed as we drew deeper into the mist and headed down the estuary and out to sea.

The fog ahead started to thin, so we turned the throttle, moving higher in the water as the steady drone rose an octave and came fully to life. Then we were through the last trailing patches of mist, lifting the nose of the craft higher as we sped through the morning, now fully alive as we clutched tightly to ropes and raced towards our destination. Then, as if surprised to find us at that hour of the day, a lone seagull appeared at our prow, swooping once with a piercing cry of protest — or was it welcome? — and then turning to head back towards the town.

Now that we were clear of the mist, we could see that we were not in fact alone. A dinghy manned by two anglers rocked gently as we slowed to pass, one of the anglers nodding in our direction then turning back to talk to his friend. Another boat, larger than ours, was chugging steadily towards the estuary mouth while still another had stopped in the distance, drifting slowly so that we were just able to make out the actions of its occupants, a half-dozen or so anglers who appeared to be feathering for mackerel.

Another boat appeared at our back, but, as

Drifting over the Skerries banks.

we left the estuary itself and headed for the sandbanks beyond, so we turned on the power and soon left him behind, passing the slower boat and then drawing closer to our destination. Briefly we paused, sending tiny feathers down in an effort to catch some launce — greater sand-eels — but only one appeared amidst a flurry of mackerel that fought all the way to the surface and then slapped against the bucket into which they were dropped. Once we had collected enough, we dropped the feathers back into the tackle box and drew out our secret weapon, a pair of silver spoons to which we had added attractors — red or yellow beads — and to which we would now add half a peeler crab with its claws and three legs. Satisfied, we whipped the body quickly with elasticated thread to make it harder to remove, then lined ourselves up with the larger boat that was now drifting the banks, albeit at a respectable distance. Two sets of tackle headed steadily for the bottom, the spoons waving some 10 ft (3 m) behind a zinc bullet, and then we waited while the tips of the rods began marking the tempo of the lures. We watched intently, but they settled into a rhythmic tick-tock which we thought was just about right, so we settled back and waited patiently for bites.

For a while nothing happened, but then I saw a tug at the rod, the tip twitching gently before settling back as I flipped the baitcaster, a Ryobi T20, so that line could be taken from the reel. Nothing else happened, so I fed it some more line, picking up the rod and waiting until I once again felt a tremor. This time I swept the rod up, hitting hard into the plaice which reacted angrily, turning and running so that line was taken against the drag. The rod, a light, pistol-grip baitcaster, arched over and then bucked in my hand as I felt the power of the fish.

Each time I turned the handle, the fish fought back against the pressure from above. I would gain some line, it would take it, but each time it ran it took a little less than before, allowing me to bring it nearer and nearer.

Then, suddenly, we could see it, a prime plaice weighing about $2\frac{1}{2}$ lb (1·1 kg). It must have seen us as well for it hunched its shoulders, so to speak, and then dived for the bottom with great sweeps of the tail.

It was not ready to come, so I let it go, mindful of the light line that I was using. On 6 lb (2·7 kg) breaking strain you have to exercise great care when you bring the fish to the side of the boat, so it is not worth taking chances. Instead I brought it gradually back to the surface, to which it responded as before. Now was obviously not the time to force the issue, so I let it take line once again. The third time it was too tired to resist as we drew it to the side of the boat, took hold of the trace and then handlined it closer to the net. In it went and then we swept it aboard, killing it quickly with a priest that we kept close to hand, then unhooking it and dropping it in with the mackerel. Both of us grinned and then lowered the tackle for another drift.

Over the course of that particular day, a few more plaice hit the lures, but they were not as plentiful as we had hoped. It certainly was not the most successful day I have ever had with the spoon, even though it was still very enjoyable. One thing it did do though was to make me take a really good look at the method to see if there was any way in which I could catch some more fish. Now I like the baited spoon and, over the years, I have caught a lot of fish on it, but I am not convinced that the tackle is perfect in the way that it is usually presented. Let me explain why. Normally, when you buy a spoon, you get two swivels, one of which is connected to a short trace and hook (see diagram on page 115). This does catch fish, but when I looked at it I was reminded of a part of J. P. Gerrard's book, *Flatfish and How to Catch Them*, in which he records that the best catches he made were when the bait simply followed the spoon without spinning. To achieve that effect he used a chain of several swivels and split rings so that the rotation of the spoon was counteracted by the swivels in the chain. He also felt that the distance the hook trailed behind the spoon was crucial, with the best results attained when the bend of the hook was following the spoon at a distance of exactly $1\frac{1}{2}$ in (37·5 mm), so he organized his tackle to do exactly that.

Now, by modern standards, the result he achieved was obviously a pretty bulky tackle, but it was also obvious that the fish were not deterred by the swivels near the hooks. He caught far too many for that to be true. No, they were interested in the movement of the spoon and the bait. Taking that into account I began to wonder what would happen if I took a modern spoon, eliminated as much of the spin as possible and then doubled the appeal of the bait by fishing two hooks instead of one.

I was reluctant to use a chain of swivels, so I experimented with a dodge used in Canada for trolling on some of their waters after trout, namely using a length of 'ball-and-socket' style bathroom chain. This is quite cheap and works in exactly the same way as several swivels but is even more efficient. A 2 in (50 mm) length, for example, virtually eliminates line twist altogether and is far less bulky, which made it a very attractive proposition.

Next came the actual spoon itself. I decided to approach this from two different angles, both of which have had a certain degree of success. For the first one I needed a Delta Sonar lure, which I rigged up in the following way. I took a 2 in (50 mm) length of chain and added a fold-over connector to both ends, just as you would if you were putting a new chain on your bath or your sink. Next I removed the bottom swivel from the spoon and connected the chain to it with the smallest split ring I could find. At the other end of the chain I used a similar split ring to attach the third eye of a treble swivel and another two to connect a size 2 Aberdeen to each of the other two eyes. The result was a virtually tangle-proof tackle that held the baits steady and doubled the amount of scent near the spoon (see diagram on page 116). So far it has worked pretty well,

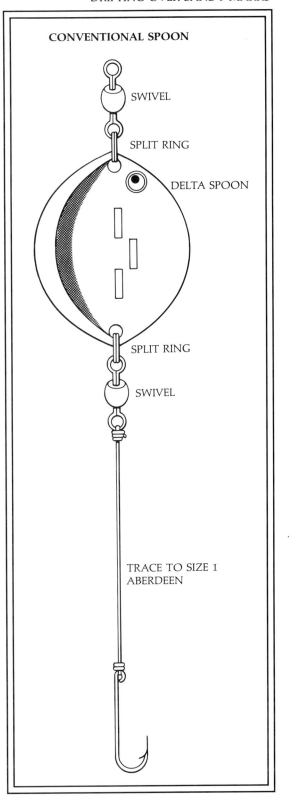

CONVENTIONAL SPOON

SWIVEL

SPLIT RING

DELTA SPOON

SPLIT RING

SWIVEL

TRACE TO SIZE 1 ABERDEEN

ADAPTED SPOON

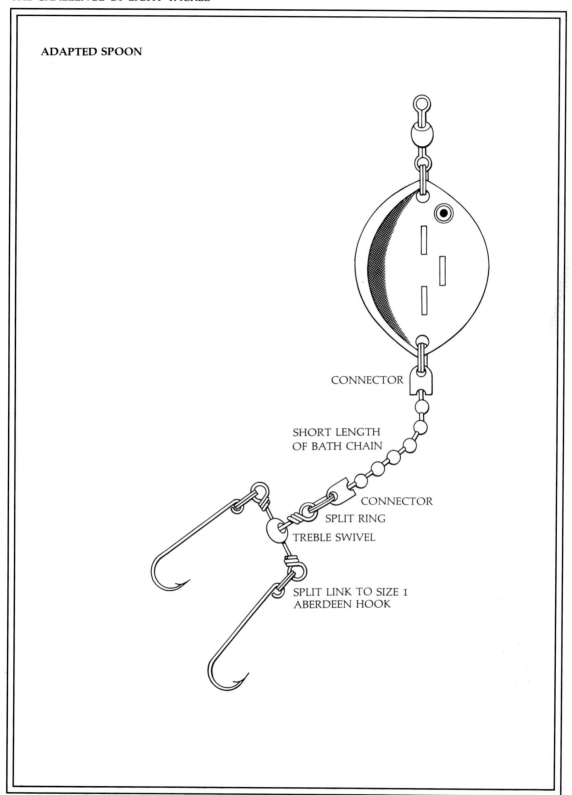

CONNECTOR

SHORT LENGTH
OF BATH CHAIN

CONNECTOR

SPLIT RING

TREBLE SWIVEL

SPLIT LINK TO SIZE 1
ABERDEEN HOOK

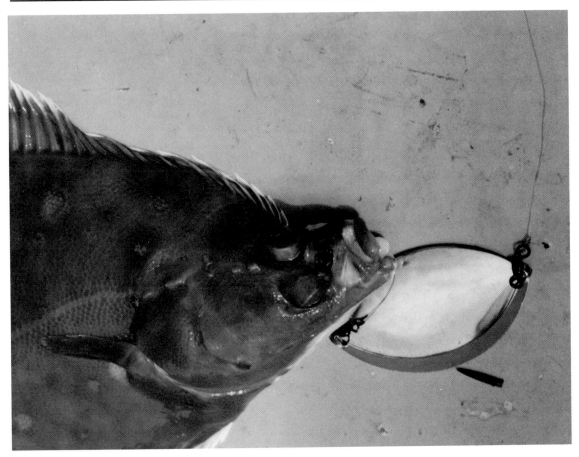

Plaice are one of the species most often caught on the baited spoon.

but I was still a little unhappy with the distance the hook trailed behind the spoon. It was closer than you could rig it with nylon, but it was still a long way off the $1\frac{1}{2}$ in (40 mm) I had hoped for.

My second approach was an entirely home-made affair. I took a metal tablespoon and used a hacksaw to remove the handle. I rounded the end with a file and then carefully drilled the resulting spoon centrally at the opposite end. A split ring was then attached, to which I connected a length of chain that was approximately $\frac{2}{5}$ in (10 mm) shorter than the spoon itself. I rigged this up exactly as previously described, with the sole exception that the first split ring also had a swivel on it (see diagram on page 118). The finished product was a lot

more compact, had an entirely different action – much closer to the spoons Mr Gerrard had advocated – and the hooks trailed at almost exactly the distance I had hoped for. Since then it has done reasonably well, but I would be interested to see how it does in other areas than Torbay, which does, after all, have the advantage of the Skerries banks close at hand.

The Skerries are, of course, justifiably famous for the numbers of plaice which they produce, but there are sandbanks near to the entrances of many, if not most, of the estuaries around the coast. Many of these can be reached with a fairly small craft as long as they are launched in the estuary and have a reasonable turn of speed. You might like to try that for yourself but I would advise, however, that

HOME-MADE SPOON

Remove the handle from an old spoon and grind it smooth. Drill a hole and attach the spoon to the split ring.

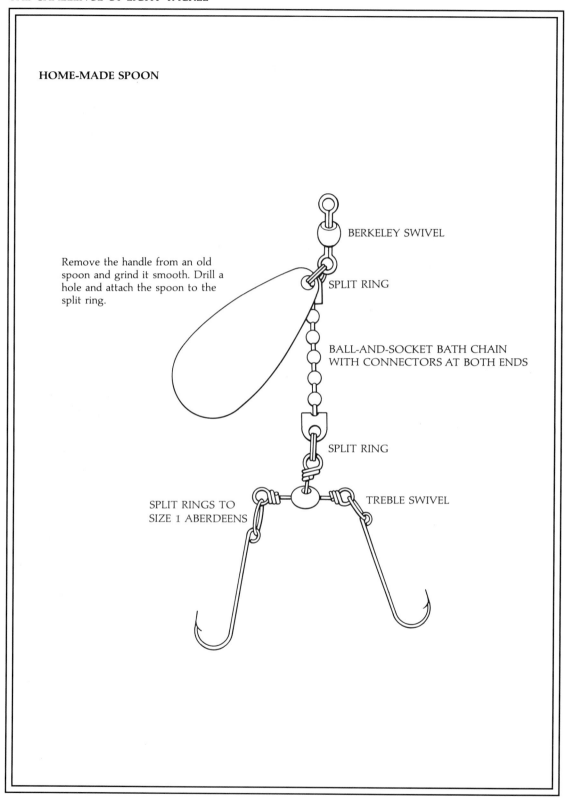

BERKELEY SWIVEL

SPLIT RING

BALL-AND-SOCKET BATH CHAIN
WITH CONNECTORS AT BOTH ENDS

SPLIT RING

SPLIT RINGS TO
SIZE 1 ABERDEENS

TREBLE SWIVEL

you get a map first of all and study it well, both before and during the time that you are actually afloat. If you can also organize your trip so that you are fishing with another boat fairly close by, that would probably be a good idea. There are some very strong tidal races on some of these marks, so that it can be very reassuring to have another boat nearby in the event that you run into problems.

There is one thing that all of these banks have in common. They provide rich feeding for a variety of species and offer the light-tackle angler a superb opportunity for getting to grips with some quality sport. Plaice and dabs are usually there in quantity, but to a lesser extent so are brill (at least on southern marks), turbot, rays, cod and whiting in the appropriate season, bass, mackerel, garfish and pollack, many of them drawn by the huge numbers of sandeels that usually live on such marks.

Taking flatfish first of all, there are several ways in which you can fish for them, but I would say the two best are the baited spoon and straightforward legering with a very long trace, certainly not less than 10–12 ft (3–3·7 m) long. This probably accounts for the best specimens caught off the Skerries each year and is arguably the best method to use. I have used it on numerous occasions, both with and without attractors, and will undoubtedly do so again.

If you decide to use attractors, you will need to put a telephone stop on your trace so that they are not more than 1 ft (30 cm) away from the hook. If you use beads, then stick to white, yellow, orange, red or combinations of the same. If you use a miniature spoon or a drilled teaspoon with the handle removed, make sure you place it between a couple of yellow micro-beads so that it stays between the stop and the hook. Alternatively you can now buy packets of unattached blades which you can slide on your line. I would suggest that you stick to only one – I have seen people with chains of them on their traces, for all the good it did them – and give it a quick polish

the day before you go fishing, washing it thoroughly afterwards to remove the scent of the polish.

I would also suggest that you stick to one hook on your leger, unless you are fishing on your own, because two hooks on a very long trace can be awfully fiddly if you get tangled with a friend. If the fish are feeding then just the one hook is all you need, especially if you have scaled your tackle down as light as you can go. For flatfish I like using a baitcaster and multiplier, set up with 6–8 lb (2·7–3·6 kg) breaking-strain line, but will step up to a stalking rod for bass, probably matched with an ABU 6500 (level wind retained) with 8–12 lb (3·6–5·4 kg) breaking-strain line, depending on the size of the fish that I expect to catch, or a 12 lb (5·4 kg) class rod if I want to fish for turbot or rays. I find these outfits give some terrific fun and are a pleasure to use, but you might also like to experiment with match rods and tiny multipliers for whiting, mackerel and garfish.

While you are legering for the flatfish, you may find your bait being taken by a bass, particularly if you are using peeler crab as bait. If that happens, then change over to live sand-eels and go back for another drift. There are occasions when bass will congregate on sand-banks in fairly large numbers. They may take the odd crab or two, but live sandeels will catch far more than peelers. The chances are that the bass are already preoccupied with the sandeels living on the banks, so it makes sense to offer them the bait that they expect to find. You may even find your sandeel being taken by a turbot or a brill, both of which will fight well and make superb eating later. If you do catch a big turbot on light tackle, then the most important thing to remember is not to rush things. I have seen more quality fish lost through people trying to bully them aboard than through anything else. If a turbot does take your bait, then the chances are – unless you struck quickly – that it will be hooked in the throat, where there is little chance of the hook coming free. Just keep steady pressure

A brace of nice plaice taken from the Skerries off Dartmouth.

on the fish and set your drag so that the fish, if it decides to run, will take line from your reel rather than snapping the line. Sooner or later it will get tired, but the danger point will be when you get it to the side of the boat. When the fish does come in sight, then guide it with the rod tip directly over its head. The last thing you want is for it to dive and snap the line with a slap of its tail added to the momentum of its dive. The point when it comes into view is often the trickiest part of the fight and you will need to be ready to give line if the fish decides to run. You may also find yourself doing this several times before the fish can be successfully boated.

Another dodge which is worth trying is to put a flyer on the main line just before the weight. This can occasionally pick up bream and mackerel along with the occasional school-ie. All you need to do is to tie a power-gum stop some 3 ft (90 cm) from the end of the main line, then slide on an Avis boom with a short trace and size 2 Aberdeen baited with live sandeel. Slide on a small float below the boom and then finish rigging up the leger as usual; the diagram on page 123 should help. The final effect is to place a livebait fairly close to the bottom, where it is visible to any number of predators. It can be very successful, particularly for large mackerel, the biggest of which often tend to hunt nearer the bottom than they do in midwater.

Sometimes it can be worth experimenting with the paternoster tackle demonstrated in Chapter 8, using traces some 12–18 in (30–45 cm) long. It is mediocre — at best — for flatfish, but during the summer it will occasionally take bream, especially if you bounce it back in the current. In practice it is at its best when the whiting first appear on the scene. When they do make themselves known, it is often in such quantity that you have little or no chance of getting through the shoals to catch anything else. This happens on the Skerries, when, for 2 or 3 weeks each year, the sandbanks seem absolutely flooded with enormous numbers of whiting. They are invariably the first fish to reach your bait and take it with an enthusiastic bite which is hard to miss. Frankly, at times such as this, there is little point in throwing away expensive peeler crab on whiting. They will take virtually any bait with gusto, but strips of fish, live sand-eels or chunks of squid are far more likely to catch the bigger ones. It is a case of 'If you can't beat them...' then you might as well make sure you catch the biggest fish that you can. If you want to stick to leger, why not experiment with a whole *calamari* squid on a pennel rig, with one hook through the head while the other is at the top of the body. If this does take a whiting, the chances are that it will be a big one, but it is also quite likely to attract the attention of any passing cod, dogfish, bull huss or even rays. Its sheer size may deter the smaller whiting — although even little ones will try to grab the head — but at least give you a halfway chance of catching something decent. You might even go for black lugworm on the hook but, if you have not dug your own, then the expense of this tactic can be moderately horrific. Frankly, I would be tempted to get out a match rod and set it up on paternoster fished very near the bottom with a decent strip of mackerel. You can get a surprising fight on this gear, with whiting about the 1 lb (0·5 kg) mark putting a very determined bend in the rod, and end up having a very enjoyable day. Why not try it and see?

Float-fishing is also an interesting method to use over sandbanks and one which is, for whatever reason, frequently neglected. It is very effective for mackerel and garfish, but it will also take the occasional John Dory, particularly in the autumn as the weather gets colder, bass, whiting and scad. Baitcasters are ideal for this type of fishing, but telescopics are also well worth investigating, especially as you can often get a lovely action from a very cheap rod. The only point to watch out for is the rings, which do tend to corrode if you fail to wipe them down after each trip. It is not a huge problem and one which is easily sorted out by just dabbing a spot of petroleum jelly around the base of the rings every so often.

Telescopics are very useful on boats because they are so convenient to store. However, on some of my friends' boats this convenience has taken the form of the rods being used for a trip, packed away and then left on the boat for the next time that they are needed. There is nothing wrong with this as long as you remember that they are in a highly corrosive environment and take steps accordingly, using petroleum jelly on the reel seat and rings and giving the reel an occasional strip-down and clean. At the very least, keep a can of WD40 handy and give the reel an occasional spray and wipe-down. If you do this you will vastly prolong its working life, especially if you keep some material handy and wrap the rod and reel after use, put it in a dustbin liner, fold the end over and then wrap the bag around a few times.

Some of the heavier telescopics – such as the DAM California Blues, matched with perhaps a Ryobi Trymaster 70CL – are also ideal for bigger fish, such as rays. They are easily stored until needed, can be left set up and, consequently, can be ready to fish in seconds. This is particularly useful when the tide starts to drop and the fish go off the feed. At such times it is well worth positioning yourself over one of the deeper holes and dropping down to see if you can get a ray. A baitcaster will be too light for this, while the heavier telescopic is still light enough to get an enjoyable struggle, especially when you get a bigger one.

For end tackle I would suggest a leger with a trace made out of 30 lb (13·6 kg) breaking-strain line. This should not be too long, certainly not over 8 ft (2·4 m) and should be baited with either a recently dead sand-eel, the head of a *calamari* squid or a half-fillet of mackerel. These will all take rays, but will also take the occasional turbot, spurdog, bull huss or bass.

One last tactic which I will mention is a device which has been imported from the USA and which, although relatively untried over here, can be very successful. It is called a 'downrigger' and is basically a means of controlling the depth at which a bait can be trolled, while also allowing the angler to use only a swivel, trace and hook. There are only a few professional models over here at the moment, but a useful one is the Cannon Sport-Troll, which is available from Normark. It is expensive, but is a well-made and sturdy item with a rod-holder already attached in the best position for actual fishing. You simply clamp or bolt the downrigger to the transom of your boat, slide your rod into the rest and Bingo! You are ready for fishing. It is also easily removable if you are worried about security, although you will need to use wing nuts instead of conventional nuts if you decide to bolt it to the transom instead of clamping it.

To use a downrigger, you simply let out line behind the boat to the distance that you want the bait to fish, keeping the boat slowly moving forward so that there is little danger of the line fouling the propeller. When your bait is far enough out, be it 20 or 80 ft (6 or 24 m) behind the boat, clamp the line into the line release on the downrigger. This is set just above a 4 lb (1·8 kg) weight which you then crank down to whatever depth you want to fish. The bait follows it down and will be trolled behind the boat at both the depth and distance that you have decided upon. It is a neat and efficient system which is useful for bass and mackerel over sandbanks, but is also brilliant for trolling in inshore waters after bass. All you need on your line is a swivel and bait – perhaps a live sandeel for bass, or a spinner for mackerel. Slip your line into the clip and then crank your tackle down to where you want it, placing your rod in the rod rest and then waiting for the action to start. If you get a bite, the fish will frequently hook itself, pulling the line free from the line release; you are then in direct contact with it, enabling you to scale your rod down to the fish that you are after, rather than ensuring that it is strong enough to deal with the size of the weight, a

LEGER AND FLYER TACKLE

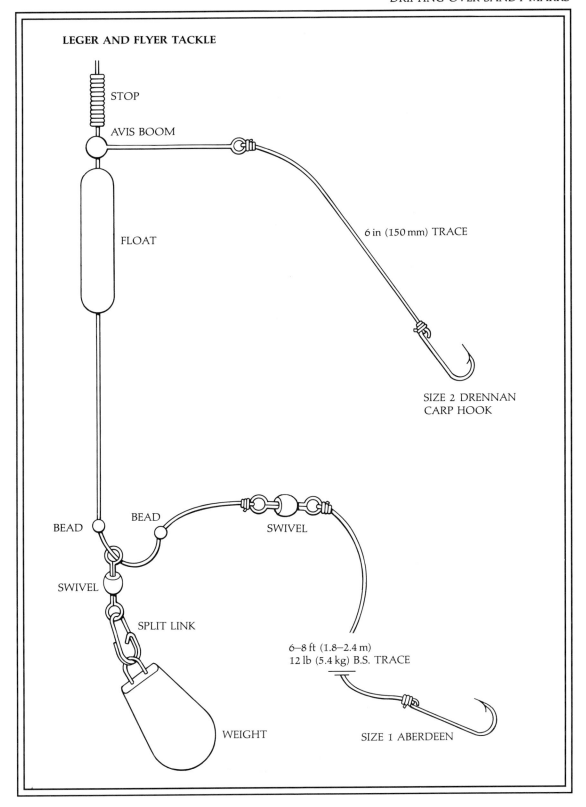

STOP

AVIS BOOM

FLOAT

6 in (150 mm) TRACE

SIZE 2 DRENNAN
CARP HOOK

BEAD

BEAD

BEAD

SWIVEL

SWIVEL

SPLIT LINK

WEIGHT

6–8 ft (1.8–2.4 m)
12 lb (5.4 kg) B.S. TRACE

SIZE 1 ABERDEEN

A specimen ray taken from a sandy mark in Torbay.

factor which you would have to consider in conventional trolling. It is a very useful method which will, I think, gain in popularity as people come to realize the control and advantages that the system has to offer. After all, instead of having to use an uptider or similar to deal with perhaps $1\frac{1}{2}$ lb (0·8 kg) of lead, you can scale your rod down to a carp-stalking rod, a baitcaster, or even a match rod if you feel that way inclined. The downrigger is handling the weight and depth while the line is held in place by a quick-release clip. This will spring loose upon contact so that you can play the fish without having its struggles masked by the heavy lead that you would otherwise have needed.

Which brings me to the final paragraph in this, the final chapter. I hope you have enjoyed the book and I hope it may have given you some food for thought.

Whether you are afloat over sandbanks or dabbling off the end of a pier, I do hope you will give lighter tackle the trial it deserves. It has the strength and sensitivity to handle the fish that you are after, while simultaneously making that fishing far more enjoyable than if you had stuck to conventional tackle. Once you get used to the feel of it, you will soon find that it will transform your fishing. With the fish stocks around our coast in the sorry state that they are in, I am more than ever convinced that light tackle is not simply a passing fad, but the best way forward for our sport to progress. Why not give it a try and see if you agree? You could well be very pleasantly surprised.

INDEX

Page references in *italics* refer to diagrams and photographs.